"We are not ... sons of slavery ... but sons of freedom under grace."

—Galatians 4:31, Phillips.

Sons of Freedom: God & The Single Man

G. H. ANDREWS

ZONDERVAN
PUBLISHING HOUSE
OF THE ZONDERVAN CORPORATION | GRAND RAPIDS, MICHIGAN 49506

To

my nephew

Jim

Unless otherwise indicated, all Scripture references are from *The Living Bible*, © 1971 by Tyndale House Publishers. Used by permission.

Scripture from *The New Testament in Modern English,* © J. B. Phillips, 1958, 1960, 1972, used by permission of The Macmillan Company.

Steve Turner, "The Conclusion," reproduced from *Tonight We Will Fake Love*, © by Charisma Books. Used by permission.

SONS OF FREEDOM: GOD AND THE SINGLE MAN
© 1975 by The Zondervan Corporation
Grand Rapids, Michigan

Fourth printing   June 1979

Library of Congress Catalog Card Number: 74-25329
ISBN 0-310-20161-6

Printed in the United States of America

Contents

Acknowledgments

This book was written with the help and encouragement of many people, especially Os Guinness, Victor Gregg, Dick Keyes, and Joe and Linette Martin, all of whom critiqued the book or parts of it and not only contributed valuable material but sometimes started a whole new train of thought going. Dr. Bill White, Professor of Psychology at the University of Pittsburgh, gave hours of his time to Chapter 11. There are others who, for obvious reasons, will not be named, whose help was inestimable on this chapter. They and I will be grateful if God uses some of their painful experiences to help others caught in the same dark web.

There were many who prayed. In the days when I thought I'd never see the end of the tunnel, their prayers made the difference.

For all these and for Judy Markham of Zondervan who spent much time cutting through tangled syntax with her expert editorial shears, for Alison Brandt who typed the final manuscript, and for Doug Heimburger who proofed it, I tender my grateful thanks to a God who makes any work in His kingdom a family operation.

Introduction

I don't want to be rude, but would you please tell me what you're doing trying to write a book for us men? I know you mean well and all that, but — well, you're not a man.

I know. And while I have no regrets about that fact, I do undertake this expedition into the territory of single men with some trepidation.

Then why do it? Why not let some man do it?

Fair questions. Some reasons:

1. There don't seem to be many books on this subject written from within a Christian framework by either men *or* women.
2. I'm attempting to give you a woman's-eye view (which I do naturally and a man couldn't counterfeit).
3. Some of you asked for it. You came and said, or you wrote, "We enjoyed *Your Half of the Apple,* but why not write a book for *us?*" At first I laughed, too. Who, me? Eventually I asked my friendly and long-suffering publisher, and he said, "Try it."

So for all of you who asked for it and for lots of you who didn't, here it is.

1

What Is Man?

Do you know who you are?

Are you having a hard time reconciling your own view of yourself with the general consensus? Man's made great advances in understanding the universe, scientific laws, and the mechanics of his own body, but today his view of himself seems waffling and uncertain. One man talks about the *ascent* of man, the next about technology *dehumanizing* man. Then along comes some so-called Christian teaching about man's being worthless.

This turns me off. Guilty, O.K., but not worthless.

Agreed. Your significance was in God's mind from the beginning. How's this for a comment on man's value: "Thou (God) hast made him little less than heavenly beings, Thou dost crown him with glory and honor. Thou givest him dominion over the works of Thy hands."[1]

[1] Ps. 8:5, 6, *Modern Language Bible.*

In giving man dominion over all other creatures, God sets a distance between man and the rest of His living creation. Even alienated from God, man retains some of the wonder of his divine origin. He thinks conceptually, makes moral choices, feels deeply. He has conquered the highest mountain, walked in space, and left machinery on the moon. From fleas to elephants, he has established dominion over the living creatures. Rocks and liquids, metals and atoms have become things of open wonder in his hands. Every day the growing edge of his knowledge moves.

But today's thinking certainly doesn't see the individual as too significant.

For a fact. Twentieth century man sees himself evolved by chance and maintained by an irreversible system. As for a relationship with a personal God, this possibility is classified with belief in Santa Claus and Snow White's seven dwarfs. As machines threaten his individuality and logic fails to give him answers, contemporary music, art, theater, and fiction either underscore man's despair over life's absurdity or offer him ephemeral solutions that disintegrate as he reaches out for them.

Take the brilliant "Mass" which Leonard Bernstein wrote for the opening of the Kennedy Center in Washington, D.C. The young Celebrant, overwhelmed by the unbelief and cynicism of the crowd, loses his own faith in the ritual and smashes the sacraments. His spiritual leadership runs out like the wine from the shattered glass. Yet suddenly, in what Bernstein calls a "reaffirmation of faith," all the young people are embracing, brotherhood replaces rebellion, obscenities and hate are forgotten. A groundless kinship emerges and everybody chants "Praise God!" and "Peace!" Even the audience is included in the surge of good will. But

10

on what ground? Moments before the crowd had told God they would set fire to His world if He didn't hurry up and change things their way. No revelation had come; nothing had been said of God's reality or the reality of the sacrifice the priest had been celebrating. The young rebels see the Celebrant as a failing human being; he sees them with new understanding — sees himself as they are. That is all. It is a stunning piece of theater and has an exciting musical score, but it offers no answers to man's real dilemma. Yet it has been called a challenge to the "place and function of religion in a world of violence" (which, in one sense, it is), offering a statement of "hope or reconciliation" (which one must question).

The Christian man, knowing who he is, can begin to understand his role in relation to others. God's communication to him sets guidelines for his life.

He knows he is to respect and honor his parents and that God expects him to make this one of his primary responsibilities.

If he marries, his responsibility to his wife takes precedence over this but does not abrogate it. Scripture clearly defines his role in relation to his wife and children.

Implicitly and explicitly, the New Testament tells him about loyalty, unselfishness, and helpfulness in a wide variety of social interchanges (e.g. friends, neighbors, business associates).

His link with other Christians is real and involves a special responsibility of love he cannot ignore. Not all Christians will be equally close. There is freedom to choose close friendships, but all Christians are related in the same family.

In the church structure he may or may not have a position of leadership, but all Christians are told to be subject to each other. No despots.

If he acquires enemies, he's not to waste energy on

11

hate or on plots for revenge. He is to love them and pray for them. (Everyone knows this in theory; living it out is another matter.)

In relation to the larger world, he has a responsibility toward need and injustice in all forms. He is to care not only for men's "immortal souls," but also for their very mortal bodies, their loneliness, their housing, their heartaches, and their food. For the *whole man.*

Governments are to be his concern. If he is not personally involved, he has the responsibility to pray.

His environment is important to him. It is God's world he's living in. If man abrogates his position of responsibility for earth and its creatures, he is in trouble individually — but so is his world. His idea of dominion has too often been an autonomous I'll-do-it-my-way that has resulted in exploitation of some animal species to extinction, consumption of natural resources to the point of no return, and pollution of the air until he threatens his own existence.

I don't feel too comfortable about all this. In fact, I feel inadequate.

Self-acceptance is a basic concept isn't it? Until he understands who he is before God, the Christian man is caught in the contemporary confusion over identity, leadership, authority, and role definition. "Christ has brought you into the very presence of God, and you are standing there before him with nothing left against you — nothing left that he could even chide you for."[2] "(You are) heirs of God, and joint heirs with Christ."[3]

Me?

You. Understanding who you are before God can

[2] Col. 1:22.
[3] Rom. 8:17, KJV.

12

do much to help you understand your horizontal roles.

But I'm sure not living a sinless life.

Who is? Learning how to reconcile the theological *position* with day-by-day living is a challenge all Christians face. Most of us know all too well the agonizing tension Paul felt: wanting to do good and not able to; hating the evil he found himself doing.

Christian growth, like all growth, is slow-motion. God's not looking for supermen but for those who'll allow Him to make them into men like His Son.

But to be frank, we younger men look around, and we don't see many examples to follow.

Ouch. That hurts. Still, if you can't find an example, *be* one. Timothy was young, but he was told to be an example to other believers in word, action, love, spirit, faith, and purity.

Large order.

Sometimes God will give you the inspiration of examples, and the Bible is full of challenging ones. But your supreme example of a true man in a man's role is the Lord Jesus Christ Himself.

Has it occurred to you that you men may have an advantage over us females?

One? I can think of several.

You would.

Well, aren't we bigger — stronger?

Usually.

More logical?

Sometimes.

Steadier?

Are you?

Less emotional?

Really? Remember the time Lucy borrowed your car and dented —

That! Emotional! I went bananas! I mean there are times —

Exactly. But now let's get serious.

You were saying something about an advantage.

There are two ways of identifying with Christ: on the human level — the perfect man who understands us completely, and on the divine level — united with Him in His risen life. Because He was a man, not a woman, you men may be able to identify with Him even more closely than we women. He lived in a totally normal male body. His *humanity* makes it possible for all of us to identify with Him, but your outlook was His in a *particular* way.

Scripture says that He is not someone "to whom our weaknesses are unintelligible — he himself has shared fully in all our experience of temptation, except that he never sinned."[4] Do you believe that?

Of course, I know He was human, God in a man's body.

[4] Heb. 4:15, Phillips.

But He WAS superhuman. After all, He never sinned. Whereas I —

It does say He never sinned. But try substituting "my" for "our" in that quote from Hebrews: "He's not superhuman in the sense that *my* weaknesses (name them) are unintelligible — that He is unable to understand or have a fellow-feeling for *my* weaknesses and liability to assaults of temptation (be specific here). He Himself shared in all *my* experiences of temptation."

You can't mean ALL?

What *I* mean doesn't count, does it? It's what God says in His revelation to us. And He does say *all*.

Somehow I find that Christ as a man seems remote, unreal. I can't seem to relate.

The man Christ Jesus has become obscured. I think it's important for us to ask the Holy Spirit to strip away the trappings of a false tradition which clouds our concept of Jesus as man. When you are told you are to be like Christ, that the aim of your life as a Christian man is to be Christlike, what is your reaction? Honestly.

If you put it that way, I suppose my gut reaction is that I don't really want to be what you'd call meek or saintly or mild. For me, those qualities don't define a real man. I feel a little guilty I guess, but — you asked for it — there it is.

Many of us find this difficult, but for you young men it must be especially hard. Part of the reaction is   15 one's own inherent rebelliousness against purity or holiness, but much of it has to do with a wrong impression of what Christ was in reality. Through several hundred years Satan has scored an immense victory in the pictorial representations of Jesus that have come down to us. We must attribute to many of the painters and sculptors, even some of the best of them, our idea of a pale ascetic, totally withdrawn from everyday life, with no appeal to the average adult and one from whom any normal child would run and hide. In our own day we have the vacillating weakling of *Jesus Christ, Superstar* or the blasphemous, bisexual character the Danes are trying to portray in their controversial movie, *The Life and Loves of Jesus Christ*. Make no mistake: Satan is still doing a highly successful "anti-Jesus" propaganda job. There are thousands, if not millions of young people in many countries whose only "understanding" of Christ is going to be obtained from distorted film and theater versions.

In Paul's day, God's fighting men faced lions. Today, no lions, but as God's militia you are asked to *demonstrate* what He is like. How can you do this if your own view of Christ is unconsciously watered down, emasculated, and canonized into unreality?

2

Royal Revolutionary

Jesus, the man, was a blazing revolutionary. He has not survived 2000 years, changed history, overturned governments, and transformed human lives because He was the "gentle-Jesus-meek-and-mild" of the Sunday school calendars.

In our sincere efforts to defend the concept of His deity and to counteract the viewpoint that Jesus was merely a "good man" (an option not really open, by the way), I think we Christians have lost sight of His magnificent humanness. God incarnate He most certainly was. If this were not so, we would have no basis for our Christian faith. But in order to appreciate Him as a relevant prototype for today's man, we may need a fresh look at Him as a human being.

Christ began His active public ministry when He was several years older than many of you — thirty. Some of you have been to Israel; all of you have read about it. You know the terrain and the climate. Visualize Him there. No planes, trains, or cars. As far as I know, the only ride He ever got on land was on a borrowed donkey. Walking over that parched country in the tropical sun did not produce the wan Christ of the medieval paintings.

Mild? Yes, He could be mild with the strength it takes to be gentle when confronted with weakness or stupidity. Many remarks made to Him would trigger our tempers like a lighted dynamite fuse. Certainly there were temptations to retaliate with violence, but His attitude toward people was impeccable. In a strong man, gentleness is beautiful. Children, always quick to differentiate between kindred spirits and phonies, found Him attractive. I can imagine His stooping to pick up a bird with a wounded wing or touching an animal in pain.

I can appreciate these things, but I still have some trouble visualizing Him as a "masculine man" as we define the term today. It's not that I disbelieve. Maybe it IS visual brainwashing.

I can empathize. It might make an interesting rap session if some of you men would thresh out what you feel constitutes manliness today and then check these concepts against the man Jesus.

For instance, strength and physical fitness are important to most of you. Right?

Right.

The eighteen years Jesus spent in Joseph's carpentry shop would not have produced a weakling. He walked and climbed miles of bad roads in all kinds of weather. And He never used His supernatural powers for His own advantage.

I think moral stamina is important. He certainly had that.

Yes. During the lonely and terrifying days of His temptation in the desert who knows what deep struggles and anguish Jesus had to go through to accept the life of intense suffering and self-denial that was to be His? "And even though Jesus was God's Son, he had to learn from experience what it was like to obey, when obeying meant suffering."[1]

Forty days, forty nights, tempted by Satan. The setting was the rock-strewn desert — an inferno by day and cuttingly cold after sundown. Jesus was a man, with a body and an emotional nature like your own. For more than a month He heard no human voice, touched no hand, saw no friend. Day after day the battle raged with His ancient adversary ("I beheld Satan as lightning fall from heaven"[2]). Here was Lucifer again — scheming and plotting His overthrow. The devil did not delegate this mission to any minion or even to one of his "great evil princes of darkness"; he was there in person. And at the end, when Christ was at His weakest, Satan moved in for the big assault.

Christ as man had taken the position of dependence on His Father, a model for all future sons of the kingdom. Satan attacked this dependence: *Assert Yourself. Show who You are. Play the game MY way. Use MY tools.* With his own diabolical ingenuity, he drew up his artillery. Using the three vulnerable areas John commented on years later, he first tried the flesh: "Tell this stone to become a loaf of bread." When that failed, he appealed to the eye: "I will give you all these splendid kingdoms and their glory." They were his to give: beauty, possessions, houses, lands. Finally the offer was power: *Jump off!* Five hundred feet high that pinnacle was. *Power, success, adulation — Jerusalem — even the Romans — will be at Your feet. Think what You could accomplish for God with this power.*

---

[1] Heb. 5:8.
[2] Luke 10:18, KJV.

Christ's weapon was the same available to the simplest believer in the family. He did not argue with Satan (something we need to remember in our own battles with the Evil One). Quietly and firmly He used the authority of His own written Word.

Weakness? Uncertainty as to who He was? Do you know of any other man in history with moral fiber like that?

In daily contacts His courage was extraordinary. There He was — a young man, minus background, social status, or diploma from any recognized Jewish school, sending a message to Herod: "Go tell that fox . . ." (Herod, mind you, the local "godfather" who had just lopped off a man's head to satisfy an immoral woman's whim). Or relive the scene when this young "nobody" from Nazareth walked into the Temple:

He looks over what has become a Chicago-stock-yard-cum-Wall-Street-Exchange. Here is big business at work, and all the more impressive because it is church work. All the familiar types are here: the successful financier, rubbing his hands and keeping a sharp eye on all those booths that are part of his syndicate; the little boothkeeper, worried and anxious: "There comes the boss, and business has not been good — not good at all. The opposition's been getting all the best pigeons." The clink of money is audible. A poor widow pleads for a better price on the cheapest offering available — two turtledoves. "Sir, I don't have that much, and I must — *must* make the sacrifice today. God wants —" "Sorry lady. No matter what God wants, *my* boss wants that price. If you don't have it, sweat it out."

In walks a sunburned figure. He stands at the entrance awhile, watching, unnoticed by the crowd — least of all by the trade czars. The rather scruffy group with Him watches anxiously, a bit awe-struck by the magnificence of the structure, the smell of big business

20

and power. Sun slants on the glittering piles of coins, birds squawk, hawkers hawk, people shout, a few cry.

Suddenly . . .

"What's He doing?" The followers begin to worry.

The Master is busy with some cords He has picked up somewhere. Knots, wrappings, more knots. The strong hands of the carpenter are skillful.

"Master?"

They look at His face and are still. They have not seen *this* face before. The eyes they have known as serene, tender, even probing flash like lightning. With a stride of authority, indignation pouring from Him like fire from a flame-thrower, He drives the businessmen right and left. The tables are hurled to the marble floor. Coins roll in every direction.

"My accounts! My accounts! I'll be fired! I'm ruined!" the wizened little man with the avaricious face cries in anguish. Doves flutter free in clouds and seek refuge high above the screeching mob. Sheep and oxen, noisily vocal, stampede from the evil-smelling court.

"Get these things out of here." The voice! Like Sinai! "Don't turn my Father's House into a market!"[3]

Meek? Mild? Or — Emmanuel — God with us?

I wonder if any of us can understand the courage it took for Jesus to go on to Jerusalem when He knew so well what was waiting there: the closeted schemers, the spying, the cruelty of the Roman mind that had devised crucifixion, the quisling in His own ranks. "He moved steadily onward towards Jerusalem with an iron will."[4]

There was day-to-day bravery as well. For three-and-a-half years He encountered hostility, mockery, and unbelief: the cold-eyed Pharisee, the cynical Sadducee, the common man out for what he could get, opting out when the crunch came.

---

[3] John 2:16.
[4] Luke 9:51.

As the world judges leadership, He was a failure. He surrounded Himself with a band of twelve no-bodies: fishermen, a revenue agent working for the occupation forces, a thief, and a gaggle of others. At His trial and execution, where were they? What kind of leadership was that? Yet His resurrection metamorphosed eleven men into tigers for God, into those "who have turned the world upside down." (Judas, realizing it was Christ as God or his own road's end, had chosen suicide.)

Today every country on earth acknowledges Christ's existence as it dates letters, books, periodicals, and newspapers. Millions of His followers have formed a singing procession for 2000 years. Men have died for love of this man whose life had seemed to end in disgrace on a Roman invention of torment.

As He traveled through the Jewish towns, ". . . the crowd . . . listened to him with great interest."[5] Women, one of them from Herod's household, knew that here was someone who understood. Braving ridicule, they came for healing and forgiveness, pouring out devotion and perfume. What quiet authority and love His voice must have had! A word, and people just packed up and left their jobs: fishermen their nets, Matthew his scroll-cluttered desk. Two followed out of curiosity: "Where do you live?" — an ordinary question. "Come and see." And their lives were never the same. A man under a fig tree, another who knew the prophets, and one man so short he had to shinny up a tree to get any kind of view. A courtesan in a Samaritan city, Roman commanders and wealthy Jews — all kinds of people fell under the spell of this man who was "only a carpenter" in His hometown.

You don't want to be like the man whose "picture" you've seen in art galleries? I don't blame you. *That's*

---

[5] Mark 12: 37.

not Jesus. Thread through the gospels. Find the warm, commanding presence who drew deep lessons from common things: wheat, sand, and fish; who gave Himself till there was no time to eat; who spent all night in prayer and when confronted by another crowd (hot, smelly, dirty, and disease-infested), could not send them away. This is your prototype.

Christ spoke of various human roles in the pithy way that was characteristic of Him. His usual method of teaching was to throw out a seminal idea and leave men to ponder and make their own deductions. He did not embellish. He spoke of dutiful sons and rebellious sons. Childless, He demonstrated the tenderness of a father in His own attitude toward children. He touched on the concern of friends and brothers for each other. Stewardship was mentioned, as well as citizenship and taxpaying. He did not speak much about marriage, but what He did say covers considerable ground.

In light of the misunderstanding and attacks on Christianity's influence on "women's position" today, it might be interesting for you to study Christ's attitude toward women. In His day, women had little status. Jewish men did not even speak to their own women in public. Remember the gentle courtesy in the Lord's treatment of Mary Magdalene? And Simon, the Pharisee, was shocked when Jesus permitted Mary of Bethany to anoint His feet; Simon decided Jesus wasn't much of a prophet if He didn't know what kind of woman *she* was. Jesus knew. But He saw the *person* there — one of such infinite value that He was going to die for her in a short time. In everything He did, Christ recognized the reality of the human being made in God's image. He exhibited true humanity.

Adam, communicating with his Creator, must have understood his own position before God, his uniqueness, his partnership with his helpmeet, his control of   23 nature. In the Fall he lost all but the fragments of his likeness to his Creator. Work became a burden, and he lost his sense of identity. We are familiar with identity crises that occur when marriages break up, when jobs change, or when we are uprooted geographically. What must have been Adam's situation! Alienated from his God, barred from the only home he had ever known, he must have wondered, "Who am I now?"

When God became man it was for more than a death or atonement. Though that was central, it was accomplished in several intense, agonizing hours. He came here as an infant in humble circumstances, grew up with simple people, and spent three-and-a-half years ministering in a servant's capacity. Lonely, working long hours, tired and hungry, thirsting at a foreign well, misunderstood even by those nearest — why did He do it? In its most profound sense we'll never understand, but one of the things He did was to demonstrate what humanness was intended to be: in character, in attitudes, in relationships, in dependence on the heavenly Father.

We are to draw our identity from Christ — is that what you're saying?

Exactly. In basing your identity on Him, you are not struggling with a hazy "religious" concept; you have a person as a model in almost every major phase of human experience. The true "image of the invisible God" has appeared, and we see what man is meant to be. For us, this involves two levels: an understanding of His manhood and a daily experience with the risen Christ *today*. It's a challenge to discover what being identified with Him does mean.

Have you ever asked yourself, What *is* my identity? On what am I depending for the sense of who I am?

People often unconsciously rely on what others reflect back to them. This is not what God wants for His family, but all too often we, too, are caught on this false identity base.

I don't think I am. I don't let people's ideas of me change me.

Are you sure? Here are some possible bases on which a man can rest his identity:

1. *Status.* Are you seeing yourself as the guy with the biggest boat? Top man on campus? The man always seen with the sexiest chicks?

2. *Performance.* Are you depending on your sales record for your ego support? Basketball star? Top student? Office Romeo?

3. *Appearance.* You can go to opposite poles here. Maybe you've been eyeballing yourself in shop windows as you wheel downtown in your muscle machine — How do I look, man, how *do* I look! Or yours may be a reverse snobbery: sloppy clothes, matted hair and beard, and feet a grape-treader would sneer at.

Some of these things are O.K. per se. I have nothing against beards and long hair; in fact, I like them. But we're talking about *identity.*

Some of these things hit home, but I don't think my identity is what's at stake.

Well, do you ever get upset when someone challenges that role of yours, even inadvertently? (Someone gets a *bigger* boat; you make a bad play in basketball; you're not on the top ten for grades; your car gets smashed up. Or someone criticizes you, makes you look ridiculous, takes your girl.) No one likes these things to happen, but if you find yourself becoming hostile or eaten with envy it may be more deeply rooted than momentary anger or humiliation. Your whole identity is threatened *if* it's resting on people's response to you or your own self-image. Underneath whatever facade you wear, you may be wondering: "If I'm *not* the best ballplayer, big man in the field, the man with the great vibes, *who am I?*" If your role defines who you are, your identity boat can be rocked by waves other people make.

The Cross is the ultimate statement of man's immense value to God. Having accepted God's solution to man's alienation from Himself, you have an integration point: your sonship with God through Jesus Christ.

You can accept yourself because God accepts you and because your real guilt has been forgiven on just grounds. You can know you are loved. Since your acceptance is not based on your performance but on Christ Himself, it is there for you to come back to each time you flounder.

God says you have become a new person. You are not the same any more. You are:

— accepted (Who doesn't want acceptance?)

— given the mind of Christ (Your spiritual insight is beyond that of people more brilliant than you because ". . . only those who have the Holy Spirit within them can understand what the Holy Spirit means. Others just can't take it in.")[6]

— made the righteousness of God in Him.[7]

Now since these statements are what God says about you, since this is what He reflects back to you, you can hold your head high in the light of God's love[8] and live with confidence. "If God is for us, who can be against us?"[9]

---

[6] Eph. 1:6, KJV; 1 Cor. 2:14.
[7] 2 Cor. 5:21, KJV.
[8] Rom. 5:11, Phillips.
[9] Rom. 8:31, Phillips.

Who are you? A prince with God, that's who you are. And when things go wrong and you feel so low that a snake could crawl over you, keep remembering this as *fact*. It's not where you *ought* to be; it's the place to which God Himself has elevated you. You're His man.

Because of these things, there should be a qualitative difference in the Christian life style. God says of the non-Christians: "They live blindfold in a world of illusion, and are cut off from the life of God through ignorance and insensitiveness."[10] Now just so you don't get smug about the life God's given you, He reminds you "there was a time when some of you were just like that." Now that you've been made light, your lives are to show *by contrast* how dreary and futile worldly things and attitudes are. "It is even possible (after all, it happened with you!) for light to turn the thing it shines upon into light also."[11]

How's your light quotient? Are you still in the gray limbo between two worlds? Have you thought about differences in Christian and non-Christian priorities? How much has your identity, your ego-support, changed since you became a Christian? Your new identity should permeate every facet of your life. Does it show? With Christ as the dynamic center of life, there should be a powerful chain reaction that affects every stratum of your life.

Your value systems are bound to undergo some major revisions because life has a different orientation. It's not to be, "What's in it for me?" Self-fulfillment becomes a by-product, not an end in itself.

Living for God instead of for self is bound to bring repercussions in our dealings with our fellow-man. Do we see *all* men as our brothers, *equally* created in God's image? Racism and social distinctions have no

---

[10] Eph. 4:18, Phillips.
[11] Eph. 5:13, Phillips.

part in a Christian's life. We cannot live stratified lives; we must not have one set of rules for Sunday and another for "everyday" living.

The spiritual and practical are tightly interwoven. Talking to a man about his soul if his heart is full of turmoil over a broken romance or if his stomach is empty is not good enough. The Lord met men's needs as He found them. If they were hungry, He did not deliver homilies on salvation; He fed them.

Our love must be the real thing. The alcoholic, the prostitute, the drop-out, and the drug addict know too well the phony ring of counterfeit love. They do not have to test it by biting the coin.

But is all this possible for an ordinary man like me? Even a redeemed man? Can it work?

What about Paul? He didn't live just a "devotional" life; he was very human. He lived where the action was. He seems to have been neither prepossessing in appearance nor in oratory. ("He sounds big, but it's all noise. When he gets here you will see that there is nothing great about him, and you have never heard a worse preacher.")[12] For his day, he was a veritable Kissinger when it came to travel, but with no advance reservations or preferential treatment. He could not have felt like a super-celebrity when he was slung down a wall in a basket. He experienced floods, thieves, shipwreck, mobs, deserts, and treachery from his so-called brothers in Christ. Hunger and thirst and cold. Practical, down-to-earth considerations, these. Was he stronger than you?

Paul found that it was when he was *weak* that he was strong, not the other way around. He certainly knew what it was to be "down" — "We are pressed on

[12] 2 Cor. 10:10.

every side by troubles. . . . We are perplexed because we don't know why things happen as they do (Familiar?), but we don't give up and quit. . . . We get knocked down, but we get up again and keep going."[13]

Paul seems to have been as knowledgeable about sports as he was about poetry. He was a scholar, but he worked with his hands—making tents—and his orders weren't for pup tents. Whole families lived in tents then, and it must have been tough, unwieldy work. This man, educated beyond most of his contemporaries and far beyond most of the people to whom he wrote, called himself the bond-slave of Jesus Christ.

In the final analysis, this is the point to which we each have to come. Discipleship means a willingness to be drained dry, to spend and be spent, to recognize that what we are as Christians will depend on how far we are willing to go. To model our lives after Christ or after Paul ("as I follow Christ") may seem beautifully idealistic, but the nitty-gritty can be tough.

---

[13] 2 Cor. 4:7, 9.

3

The King's Men

Being a man in today's relativistic society is no cinch. What's hard is coping on the everyday level.

The Christian life has to start with the vertical relationship. It's the "beginning of wisdom." This means much more than the initial confrontation, the "conversion experience," being "saved," or whatever your term is for becoming a Christian. It's the branch vitally connected to the Vine, remaining so intimately connected with the Source that His life runs through us into the lives of others. We often start at the wrong end of the plant, trying to produce fruit with no juices flowing. Living in Christ presupposes that the Lord is very personal. Are you experiencing His friendship? Do you know Him as someone who wants to be involved in all that interests you?

This smacks of dependency. I'm a man. Can I equate this reliance on Christ with my masculinity?

Manliness and dependence on Christ are not in conflict. In fact, *only* dependence on the Lord guarantees a lack of dependence on others. Christ's Lordship presupposes subjecthood: Either you're boss of your life or He is.

There's something still deeper, however — close relationship with Christ Himself. Today we use that word "relationship" like a chant. We're all talking about relationships: good, bad, quality of, number of, kinds of. What about your relationship with the Lord in an intimate sense?

Are you sure you're not emphasizing a strongly feminine point of view?

Fair question. We could phrase it this way: "Is a warmly personal experience with God consistent with masculinity?" If you think about it, I imagine most of you know many virile men whose Christian lives are proof of their dependence on God. The inescapable essence in the life of the great of the Kingdom, from Enoch to our own day, is that they *knew* God.

Take David for example — one of the Bible's more vigorous characters. He was a man with great charisma. Loved by all Israel and Judah, admired then hated by Saul, attractive to women, he was a man who became a legend in his own time — a fighter *and* a lover. Loyalty to him took three tough soldiers through enemy lines just to bring him a cup of water. He had a strong character streaked with contradictions: warmly compassionate but capable of flaming out in ungoverned passion and cruelty. Scripture does not whitewash the extremes of an almost larger-than-life nature.

A motley crew of vagabonds followed him to the cave of Adullam. It's not hard to imagine the dark faces lit by campfires, David playing his lute and singing his songs. Words the world has loved for centuries were

31

heard there for the first time. Eventually those gypsies became a formidable army. Why? They had been with David, the man after God's own heart.

But he had a man murdered just to cover up his own adultery — one of the bravest men from the cave days at that.

And it has marred David's image for all time. But in spite of this, the Lord seemed to concentrate on the set of David's life. Failures aside, and they were black, God was his integration point.

David's life was action-packed: son-in-law to the king but playing a deadly game of hide-and-seek among the rocks; acting the lunatic before a foreign king; betrayed by his favorite son; eventually reigning in power and wealth for forty turbulent years.

Without his songs and his prayers we could never know the heart of this man. He poured out a cascade of words, glittering with praise, warm with tears, flowing into our modern lives as if the words had just been written.

David saw God's hand in everyday living. "Now in your strength I can scale any wall, attack any troop."[1] Professional soldier that he was, he was not embarrassed to come to God for comfort and help. "Protect me as you would the pupil of your eye; hide me in the shadow of your wings as you hover over me."[2] He had a vital face-to-face relationship with God. "My heart has heard you say, 'Come and talk with me. . . .' And my heart responds, 'Lord, I am coming.' "[3]

Many of his songs demand "Why Lord?" but end in praise. He threw his confusion on God. "For I am overwhelmed and desperate, and you alone know

---

[1] Ps. 18:29.
[2] Ps. 17:8.
[3] Ps. 27:8.

which way I ought to turn. . . ."[4] He seems to sum up his whole philosophy when he says, "Lord, I put my trust in thee; I say, 'Thou art my God.' My fortunes are in thy hand."[5]

One reason God gives us such a long history of a very human man may be to show us He cares about all the details of a life. And our God has no favorites.

If you mean business with God about being a successful Christian, there are your friendships to consider. Thought much lately about who you hang around with? A man who is seldom with his fellow-Christians can easily become like a single coal removed from a hot bed of embers: the coal soon cools off.

I've experienced that, but just now my problem is finding Christian friends as intellectually stimulating as my non-Christian friends.

That's a real problem that many struggle with. It's been so discouraging for some that they've put their priorities topside-down and chosen stimulating company over family ties. The two things are not mutually exclusive. How hard have you tried to find interesting Christians in your field? Write the authors of books you find stimulating. Find out about Christian communities where people use their brains and talents. Many professional groups (doctors, musicians, scientists, etc.) have Christian discussion groups. It may take some sleuthing on your part, but if you really set about it prayerfully God may lead you to people on your own wavelength. *Don't try to live without Christian fellowship,* even if the fellowship available is less than ideal. None of us are strong enough to go it alone. This has always been true, but never more so than

---

[4] Ps. 142:3.
[5] Ps. 31:14, 15, *New English Bible.*

now when the consensus beats on our sensibilities every hour we're awake.

The Book of Proverbs has truths in it as relevant to the twentieth century man as the front page of today's *New York Times*. It emphasizes studying, searching, seeking. For wisdom, for knowledge. In an experience-oriented age, we need to rethink this question of knowledge.

Knowledge of God Himself is the beginning. We often feel we have this knowledge just because we are Christians. But becoming a Christian is only the introduction. It takes time, real desire, and effort on our part to begin to know God. It's a lifetime pursuit.

We need knowledge of His Word. Paul's admonition to Timothy about studying so he would not be an embarrassed Christian is quite contemporary. A few glib Scripture verses which come out as if someone had pressed a button, pat answers given without regard for the man we're talking to — these things don't make us well-equipped Christians. We need to be careful that we're not giving answers to questions no one is asking.

The Scriptures give us some clearly defined characteristics of God's men: trust in God in every department of life — financial, emotional, social, physical; acceptance of trials with grace, knowing God is still in control; an absence of conceit; and truthfulness. Lying for convenience, the social lie, the "compassionate" untruth — all these have become so acceptable in our society that we hardly think about them. Yet when God lists seven things He *hates*, lying is mentioned twice.

In a contemporary vein, an eminent non-Christian psychiatrist, O. Hobart Mowrer, considers lying a highly dangerous device. He discusses an article in which lying is not only excused but advocated as "innocent . . . quite innocuous . . . essential to contemporary living and one of the fundamental rights of man" (No less!). Mowrer takes the position that if we build up walls of deception we crumble behind them, having made ourselves non-responsible to society, and our walls disintegrate. He points out that a psychotic frequently cannot distinguish between his own thoughts and those of others. He feels someone is reading his mind. This is a convoluted way of making his life an open book. If others can read his mind, then deception is over and nothing need be hidden any more. Bearing in mind that no one starts lying with the big lies, if this extreme condition can be the result of serious deception, it's foolhardy to treat lying as a polite social pastime. Mowrer also points out that once we jettison this commandment, we give ourselves an open window through which to chuck the other nine.[6]

As always, the Bible is both practical and thoroughly contemporary. Why should that surprise us since it is God speaking? One would expect Him to write a book of *timeless* wisdom, even one which anticipates discoveries men make many years after the book was completed.

All this makes those little white lies take on a different color.

It also encompasses deception in subtler ways.

Such as?

Pretending to know things we don't know, to have things we don't have, to be something we're not. We need to examine the masks we use to cover up the real persons we are.

---

[6] O. Hobart Mowrer, *New Group Therapy* (New York: Van Nostrand Reinhold Co., 1964).

The Christian man is to let God settle his accounts. That cuts across the grain of our culture, doesn't it? On a TV program the other night the "bad guy" insolently poured water down the sleeve of the "good guy." For a minute he sat quietly, and it looked as if he were going to overlook it. Then he got up and took a beautiful swing at the bad guy who, naturally, was leveled. And I realized I was experiencing satisfaction in seeing the villain "get his." We are so conditioned by society's consensus that we expect a man to deal out physical "justice."

You're not suggesting I should let some jerk insult me and do NOTHING?

Let me just suggest that you do a serious study on what Scripture has to say about retaliation — and especially violence. God's man is primarily a man of peace. Everywhere today we're hearing talk about peace: peace in the world, between nations, in our country, in the home. Such broad issues must start with the individual. "When a man is trying to *please God,* God makes even his worst enemies to be at peace with him. . . . It is an honor for a man to stay out of a fight. Only fools insist on quarreling."[7]

Moral victories often call for more strength of character than physical ones. I think each Christian has to decide before God just where his own boundaries are in the matter of aggressiveness. He needs to know his actions are based on conviction, not reaction.

God requires self-control in His sons. "A man without self-control is as defenseless as a city with broken-down walls."[8] This would cover control of appetites, moods, tongue, temper.

---

[7] Prov. 16:7; 20:3.
[8] Prov. 25:28.

Learning to control appetites is a lifelong battle. Proverbs gets down to the earthy business of eating, drinking, and sleeping. (In another chapter we'll talk about sex.) "When dining with a rich man, be on your guard and don't stuff yourself, though it all tastes so good (!). . . . don't carouse with drunkards and gluttons, for they are on their way to poverty. And remember that too much sleep clothes a man with rags."[9]

No drinking?

While Scripture doesn't take a "teetotaling" position, it does speak strongly of moderation and mentions those who spend long hours in taverns, who "will say foolish, silly things that would embarrass you no end when sober."[10] (Remember those office Christmas parties?)

Friendship, loyalty, discretion: We all pay lip service to these qualities, but sometimes one wonders if they're getting on the "out of print" list. Can your friends depend on you? Can you be trusted with confidences? What about your parents? Proverbs comes right out and says that a son who mistreats father or mother is a public disgrace. It says nothing about whether or not the parent *deserves* respect. It is from their *position* under God that they derive their claim. (This may be the place to add that honoring and obeying are not necessarily synonymous. There must come a time when the boy becomes a man and may have to differ from his parents' ideas. Sonship is a permanent status; childhood is not.)

Handling our moods can be a way of showing consideration to others. We so often inflict our worst moods on those closest to us, vindicating ourselves by

---

9 Prov. 23:1, 20, 21.
10 Prov. 23:33.

saying: "I have to let off steam to *somebody,* and they'll understand." Isn't that backward reasoning? Those who love us should get the preferential treatment. I'm not suggesting we sprout wings around the house, but I think the Lord wants us to learn to bring our moodiness to Him. Prevention's a lot better than cure. If you see a dark mood curling up over the horizon, get before God with it before it becomes Satan's tool. And don't let failures discourage you. If a graph were to be made of the Christian life, it would not look like this ⟋ but like this ⩘

I find my hassle is with my big mouth.

Mmm. Yes. "Death and life are in the power of the tongue."[11] "Men have died for saying the wrong thing!"[12]

That's putting it on the line.

Proverbs mentions, too, that even a fool is thought wise when he keeps his mouth shut![13]
Talk of control, and we inevitably come to the verses about temper.

Here we go!

As usual, Proverbs balances the positive against the negative. After pointing out that a wise man controls his temper, knowing anger causes mistakes —

Does it ever!

---

[11] Prov. 18:21a, RSV.
[12] Prov. 18:21b.
[13] Prov. 17:27, 28.

— it says "a short-tempered man is a fool."[14] Temper
is more of a hazard for some than others. What to do?
If God says control it, then He's going to help us do
just that.

Can He deliver us all at once?

Well, He certainly hasn't done it in my case, but
maybe I've put up too much resistance. Still, I think it
may be unrealistic to expect overnight changes, whatever our besetting sins. He is *for* us, not against us, and
if we include Him in our struggle He will show us ways
to deal with it. Like avoiding situations that trigger
said temper. Noticing what sets it off. Dealing with a
gradual slow boil before it reaches the volcanic stage.
"It is better to be slow-tempered than famous; it is
better to have self-control than to control an army."[15]
How's that for a reversal of today's value systems?

Proverbs also says some things about laziness. "A
lazy man is brother to the saboteur,"[16] for instance.
There's the lad who thinks the nine-to-five routine is
for dum-dums, who sneaks in a nap on the job when
possible, and who zips off to the nearest golf course if
the boss is on vacation.

What *about* our work, whatever it is? Does our
motivation ever involve God's glory?

Any attempt to exclude our faith from our business
practices is going to result in spiritual bankruptcy.
"The Lord demands fairness in every business deal.
He established this principle. . . . The Lord despises
every kind of cheating."[17]

---

[14] Prov. 14:17.
[15] Prov. 16:32.
[16] Prov. 18:9.
[17] Prov. 16:11; 20:10.

The consensus says it's not possible to make real money and remain scrupulously honest.

From a purely human point of view this generally may be true. But the Christian must bank on God's promises. He says, "them that honour me I will honour,"[18] and I know highly successful businessmen who do not deviate a hair's-breadth from honesty. They run their businesses first for the Lord; He takes care of their success.

But after all, business was a bit different in Solomon's time. Are his ideas practical for us?

As Christians we believe that behind Solomon is God. And it's hard to find a more contemporary statement than, "It is poor judgment to countersign another's note, to become responsible for his debts."[19]

That's certainly up-to-date!

He also advocated watching your business interests closely. If God puts you in business, then be the best businessman possible. Material success is certainly not wrong in itself. If the rich young ruler had cheerfully agreed to sell what he had, the Lord might have said, "Don't bother." It's *attitude* that counts. (We say that all we have is God's, but does He even get "His portion" off the top? It's so easy to think we give God "His share," but as income and attendant expenses mount even ten percent begins to look too big to be "practical." We start rationalizing.)

On the other side of the coin, we should not put the man or organization living "by faith" into some rare-

---

[18] 1 Sam. 2:30, KJV.
[19] Prov. 17:18.

fied category. God does not call all men to live this way. Someone has to mind the store.

When all is said and done, the Lord Jesus Christ is your pacesetter. Only to the extent that His life flows in you can you possibly become the man God wants you to be. Commitment has to be total; there is no part of life or personality uninvolved.

The challenge has been thrown down by the Lord Himself. He expects you to do something about it. It's that simple. Whenever you find an area of weakness — temper, appetite, a little hedging on the income tax — He expects you to face up to it. What He does *not* expect you to do is pull yourself up by your own bootstraps. If you've "tried it before and it didn't work," maybe that's what you've been trying. He never intends for us to achieve His glittering ideals by ourselves. In our own strength the Christian life is not a struggle; it's a defeat.

"The Christ you have to deal with is not a weak person outside you, but a tremendous power inside you."[20]

The power is there. The choice is yours.

---

[20] 2 Cor. 13:3, Phillips.

4

On Whose Wavelength?

Decision-making is an integral part of life. As children, we were soon faced with deciding what to eat, what to wear, what game to play at recess. Going further in school, we chose courses, decided whether to make the hockey team or take trumpet lessons, whether to go steady or play the field. And the older you get, the more serious the choices. From deciding where to go on vacation or what summer job you want, you progress to whether or not you want to go to college, which college, what you want in a girl friend. Then come the *big ones:* what career, to marry or not to marry, and if so, whom. Every human being is confronted with such a bewildering array of choices in his lifetime that if he ever had to face them all at once, he'd be looking for the nearest high bridge.

All around one sees people attempting to cope with the decisions that face them. They base their decisions on empirical evidence or hedonism or on a wide range of opinions gathered from assorted sources. Such is the blind faith in the infallibility of computers, that if people could carry around portable ones and feed them their questions, many would undoubtedly do so. Thousands are letting their psychoanalysts be their decision-makers. Fortune-tellers are doing a thriving business. I Ching has serious followers, and astrology has replaced or become religion for an increasingly large number of people. Many big firms, otherwise entirely pragmatic in their approach to life and business, employ full-time astrologers and will make no deals without the right auguries.

As a Christian you are faced with as many decisions as the next man. You have freedom in making choices, but not total freedom. (A friend of mine defines total freedom as an astronaut, walking in space and insisting he's free to take his space suit off). You have the control of God's Word giving you defined limits. Within that framework, you have freedom to make your choices, moving in an environment of God's love and understanding with His promised help to keep you from choices that could prove disastrous. Always assuming you are willing to be kept.

Of course, your trust in God's competence to guide you will be in direct proportion to the depth of your relationship with Him.

Little children understand trust. As a young child, you may have responded simply and openly when told that Jesus loved you and would take care of you. As you grow older, the emphasis shifts, and you are engaged in establishing your own identity. You strike for independence. Life is exciting, and you are involved in the fascinating research of discovering who you are.

Somewhere the concept of God as an understanding friend may get lost. Have you reestablished the sort of trust that came easily when you were a child? Jesus said, "Therefore anyone who humbles himself as this little child, is the greatest in the Kingdom of Heaven."[1]

_____
[1] Matt. 18:4.

The contemporary concept of male decisiveness, of masculine independence has so saturated our thinking that I believe it is harder for a man to consider a close relationship with God than for a woman. This has surely been aggravated by our diminishing concept of friendship, especially between two men. All our concepts of human relationships are so tainted with the mold of Freudian thinking that almost any human friendship is suspect. A Divine-human one is even harder to conceptualize.

Now if God deals with you as a friend (Christ said He called us friends), you can trust Him to want you to have the best always. Knowing both the future and you, He understands what "best" is. You may not.

I often say to girls, "If you're considering marrying someone, be sure to find out on what basis he gets his guidance from the Lord. Since this man's decisions will be vital in your life and in the lives of your children, you'd better find out about this."

What's *your* criterion for guidance? On what do you base your life-changing decisions?

I pray.

Yes?

And then I try to get it together and decide what seems best.

How do you decide what's best?

God's given me common sense, hasn't He?

He has. Though using it is often another question
44 for any of us.

If you ask Him to help and then use your head, what else is there to do? We ARE free to make choices.

Yes, and the significance of those choices is important — something alarmingly so. As each new day begins, we have the privilege of committing ourselves to God. In doing this, we make a conscious choice which involves many small ones. God does not expect us to stand praying over whether or not to put out the trash. On the other hand, mundane choices (What do we have for dinner? Do I wash the car tonight or clean the garage?), while not earthshakers, may lead to important things. Suppose you decide to wash the car. The old bus has been dirty long enough. This is *it!* You're up to your elbows in suds when along comes Bill. You've been praying for him, and tonight he's all upset over a Dear John letter. What happens?

The car might not get washed, but I think I'd feel God had sent me an opportunity.

Your choice then would be to jettison your first choice and opt for God's. In one sense, there are *no* unimportant decisions.

One important consideration in your decision-making is whether or not your problem is dealt with specifically in Scripture. Sometimes that gives you an immediate answer. If not, there is still the question of God's *best*. Your choice of a career or a particular college can affect your whole life, take you to far countries, bring you to your future wife. There's no chapter and verse that will tell you whether to go to Oxford or Princeton nor is there a clear statement as to whether you should be a doctor or the manager of a clothing store, but to think God is not interested in these details of your life is to make Him less loving than a human father who cares about his son's life. **45**

As you approach God for direction, have a clear vision of what *you'd* like and know why. Some decisions can be discussed with experts in the field you are considering. People whose spiritual depth and integrity you trust should be included as well. Consider all aspects. For instance, if it's a business or a career you're deciding on, have you asked yourself: Am I getting into a career based on

— lying to people?

— manipulating people?

— dragging people down (physically, emotionally, spiritually)?

— pandering to a human weakness which does not happen to give *me* any problem?

Being part of a huge organization can absorb you and yours. It can gradually take over the direction of your whole life: where you live, what schools your kids will go to, what clubs you and your wife may join, who your friends will be.

The same criteria would apply for some of you who have become Christians while preparing for a certain profession or job. Sometimes God will want to guide you into another field. Have the daring to accept the challenge to change, knowing God does not waste anything in accomplishing His designs.

So I line up my options and choose.

Many people would stop there. My own conviction is that we go one step further and say, "I've done the best I can with the data I have available. Let me know if this *is* the right choice. If it's not, I choose with *You* against it."

46   Sounds simplistic.

Believe me, it's not. This is the point at which I usually discover how *un*committed my will is — how much I want my own way. And the battle is on. It's what Paul calls the "old Adam," the willful part of us that continues to try to be autonomous. The stronger your personality, the harder the battle. Letting God win is vitally important. Not just for *this* time, but because this struggle is a building block in the structure of your whole character as a man of God. (It is sad to see gifted, middle-aged Christians still making decisions on a humanistic basis.)

Whatever decision gives you a hard time is the *big decision*. What college, what job, even what girl, are not nearly as important as whether or not you can genuinely acknowledge Christ's Lordship in your life. Over and over He makes us face whether it is His choice that matters to us or our own. The heart of the matter is *love*. When our love for God outstrips our love for self and self-will, His desires become primary.

We all have much to learn about prayer. All too often we come into God's presence as if we were rushing into a shop demanding merchandise. The Bible speaks of being quiet in His presence, of approaching Him with reverence — even with awe. We are communicating with the One who designed and created the galaxies in limitless space.

A clear conscience is necessary for open communication. "Search me, O God, and know my heart; test my thoughts,"[2] is not a prayer to be spoken lightly. Yet if we expect to hear the quiet answering voice, we had better be sure the lines are clear.

And thanksgiving. How many times do we roar into the presence of God, shouting our needs and our heart-cries with no time for thanks for the hundreds of good

[2] Ps. 139:23.

things He gives us every day of our lives? How many times do we fail to thank Him for answered prayers? There are times we don't even notice when an answer comes because, like children tired of their toys, we have wandered off to some new interest and have all but forgotten we had asked.

"He . . . wondered that there was no intercessor."[3] How strange it must seem to Him, in view of the battle going on all around us, that we can be so uninvolved in the lives of others.

To feel that *every* time we pray we have to go through a formula — 1) worship, 2) confession, 3) intercession, etc. — would be to make our communication stereotyped and stiff. There are times when we offer a quick prayer to the God of heaven (telegram prayers), or we may be too overwhelmed to do more than groan. He hears. However, usually we have time to follow the general pattern of Bible prayers which always begin with an acknowledgment of the wonder of who God is. If we do this, by the time we get to our requests we are much more aware of the power of the God to whom we speak. Answers, even "impossible" answers, seem much more likely.

Devotional life and practical life should be like the two hands on a clock: they move together, interdependently. Bringing God into the decision about your new business venture blends your life into the homogenous whole God intends it to be.

God recognizes our individuality. He does not guide any two of us in exactly the same way. For some, the answer comes in a quiet inner conviction. "And let the peace of God rule in your hearts."[4] The Greek for that word "rule" is the word from which we get our word "umpire." Let the fact of His peace (or the lack of it) be the decisive factor.

---

[3] Isa. 59:16, KJV.
[4] Col. 3:15, KJV.

Sometimes God makes the circumstances decisive, and the door slams closed or swings open in an unmistakable way. Many find guidance in a particular verse. However, "your" verse needs to be well reinforced by other things, such as circumstances plus common sense, as this can become dangerously subjective.

What about signs?

There are biblical accounts of special signs being given. Most of us have had some experience with them at one time or another. The makeup, background, experience of the individual enter into it. Again, there is danger of emotionalism and subjectivity. Some people dislike the whole idea. Some have the courage and faith to ask for a specific, unusual sign. Gideon, that none-too-brave man turned by God into a great warrior, had that kind of faith. He asked God to change nature around, then asked Him to reverse the whole thing. God did as he asked. But you'd have to be sure you *have* this kind of faith, otherwise you may end up confused and possibly embittered. Don't be like the man who said, "Right. I've got faith. I'm praying that the mountain across the river will be gone by tomorrow morning." Next morning he rushed to look out. The hill was there, strong and firm as ever. He slammed the window shut and stormed, "I *knew* it would be there!"

As you pray for God's will, are you prepared for the fact that the answer could be difficult — even painful? The answer may be something quite different from what you anticipate.

If your prayer does result in pain, don't go on a super-sanctity trip and smile brightly and say, "It doesn't hurt at all. Everything's just fine." Much harm has been done to and by Christians with the attitude

49

that acceptance of God's will means undiluted joy. As Christ approached His great suffering, He approached God's will for Him. But He said, "My soul is crushed by sorrow,"[5] and asked His friends to stand by. Admitting pain or the ugliness of death or desertion is not "letting God down" or in some way betraying Him. Death *is* ugly; pain *does* hurt. Ours is a fallen world, and suffering is real. Our emotions will exact a severe price if we dam up every outcry.

Believing that God hears and will answer our requests for guidance is very important. And *time*. We make terrible mistakes sometimes when we ask God's will but get impatient. There are times when we need guidance now, this minute. If we do, we'll get it. But major decisions almost always take longer. In fact, God often teaches us valuable lessons in delayed answers.

[5] Mark 14:34.

5

They Also Serve . . .

Do you ever stop to think how much of life is spent in waiting? Not just waiting for guidance but just — waiting. It's a common denominator of all cultures, all eras. From ancient warriors frustrated by unexpected storms to modern man helplessly grounded in a fogbound plane, man has waited on the weather. In spite of modern medicine, today's woman, like her sister of centuries ago, often spends grinding hours in labor with a baby who will not be hurried. And from ambitious courtiers waiting for a slow-dying king to greedy twentieth century heirs hoping a millionaire will die, man has waited on death.

There is a drudgery sort of waiting: the gray hours in the precinct station, the missing person's bureau, the dentist's office. In cities, people spend hours in line waiting for tickets, for buses, for snail-like lanes of traffic, for teeing-off at the first green, for gas. We line up obediently at airports and wait for customs men to let us get on with our lives. Walk through a city park.

On the benches are old men and women: tired, drained
— waiting. Waiting for what? They don't know.

Our culture has produced the play *Waiting for
Godot* which underlines the hopelessness many feel
about deliverance from man's dilemma. In Menotti's
brilliant opera *The Consul*, Magda, the wife, finally
goes to pieces in the consul's reception room, screaming
her frustration in waiting — waiting — waiting. Filling
out endless forms over and over and then — waiting.

Yours is the instant generation. You grew up not
liking to wait for anything. One of the family cars
picked you up after school to take you to piano lessons,
the orthodontist, or football practice.

And what a row when mom was late!

You flip switches and get light, heat, and TV. Coffee
and tea are instant. You flip a dial and speak with
friends 3000 miles away. This carries over into larger
issues. Your contemporaries look for instant affluence,
now romance, split-second sex, flash retribution. When
the answers are not speedily forthcoming, they sink
into apathy and so-what-ness. They've tried shortcuts
around education, capsulizing twenty years of living
into three or four, riding the drug spaceship to instant
euphoria. Some couldn't even wait for death.

Is it possible that some of you may be looking for
instant Christianity?

No point in hedging — waiting is hard. David found
it so: "I have wept until I am exhausted; my throat
is dry and hoarse; my eyes are swollen with weeping,
waiting for my God to act."[1]

Some of you can't find jobs. Some may be hassled
over the marriage issue — you think you've waited
long enough. You may be engaged and feel you can't

---

[1] Ps. 69:3.

get married until parents' objections dissolve. You may have no money at all. Apartments are scarce or tenants won't move out. Even a small thing like mail can drive you wacky: letters from your girl, medical reports, a job application reply, college entrance exams, a needed check — *where are they?*

Doesn't it get any better as you grow older?

A little, perhaps. But waiting's never really easy. And it's worse if we don't know *what* we're waiting for.

I don't think I understand.

When a man puts his total life into God's hands, he finds some of his old decisiveness is gone, of necessity. He is no longer the "free agent" he was, making up his own mind and moving out only on his own initiative.

But then where does choice come in?

Waiting for God's leading and timing involves a disciplined kind of choice. It may seem easier to dash off on your own, but the Christian has chosen to put himself under the Lordship of Christ and this often involves waiting for direction. You may reach the point where *you* are "ready" but have no idea of God's direction. Or you may find yourself in a position of tremendous pressure that screams for action. In their earliest confrontation with the Egyptians, the Israelis found Pharoah's army roaring down on them and nothing at all in front of them but all that water. Right away they opted for Egypt: Bondage was better than death in the desert.

"Moses! Weren't there any graves in Egypt that you

had to bring us out *here* to die?" Considering the hot-spot they were in, Moses' reply must have seemed preposterous: "Don't be afraid." (Moses? We're trapped. We're scared witless. What do you mean, don't be afraid?) "Stand still" (With the whole Egyptian army coming! Listen to them!! Let's go. Only — there's no place to go. *Moses!*) "and *see* the salvation of the Lord which *He* will show you."

What a time to be standing still and waiting!

Are *you* there?

Are you shifting from one size-twelve foot to the other and saying, "Lord, where are you? Have You forgotten me? Better I never became a Christian. Better I had stayed back in bondage in Nebraska or even Amsterdam. Where *are* You?" And the heavens remain brass? No clear direction? Tired of hanging in there? Scared of the upcoming crisis? *You* know it's time to move out?

God's not going to forget you. First of all, remember that waiting is part of the heritage of being human. Then, just *because* it's so tough, waiting seems to have been one of God's great training devices for His people. There are at least fifty references in Scripture on waiting. If you find yourself waiting for God, you're in illustrious company:

> Abraham, with the promise of God in his hand so to speak, waited many years till all human hope had burned black.
>
> Joseph, with God's assurance of a bright future, ended up in an Egyptian prison — no Cairo Hilton. The years in prison kept him from flying too high as Egypt's prime minister.
>
> Jacob — poor Jacob! Struggling seven years for the wrong woman and then seven more to get the woman he loved.
>
> Moses "was skilled in all the wisdom of the Egyptians" (who, incidentally, were no slouches in knowl-

edge — they even did brain surgery). He spent a forty-year stint in the desert herding sheep. *He'd* been ready to go, but God sent him off to grow.

Young David, after being anointed king, went back to his sheep. God was not allowing his head to get too big for the crown that came thirteen years later. He may not have liked it any better than you do.

Daniel waited three weeks for an answer to intense prayer and fasting, only to learn that help had been on its way all that time. But God's messenger was delayed by an emissary of Satan!

Even Christ spent thirty years in seclusion before His public ministry.

We're like children who pull up the carrots to see if they've grown. We accept as quite normal the many years it takes to educate and train a man to be expert in any field: diplomacy, the Navy, bookkeeping, sports, philosophy, or art. Why should we be so unrealistic as to expect God to wave and make us into instant princes? You're interested in the *now.* God is not *un*interested in the now, but He has an overall view, and you're in the *process of becoming* what He wants you to be. He has chosen us to "bear the family likeness of His Son," and since we start out with very little such resemblance, it's not going to happen right away.

Waiting is often the crucible of faith. Abraham might never have been called the Father of the Faithful if Isaac had arrived right after God's promise. Against all odds, he remained "completely sure that God was well able to do anything he promised."[2]

There are times when it's necessary for the heat of our desire to drain out of us, to get it all in right proportion. God is too wise to give us the right thing at the wrong time.

Sometimes God needs to prepare us for what's coming. It may be something wonderful or it could be

---

[2] Rom. 4:21.

something very hard. Nowhere is the Christian life presented as a rose garden. We need to let Him get us ready for what the future holds.

Often He seems to wait till it's all but too late. We find ourselves near the edge of Nowheresville; then He comes, and we *know* the deliverance is His, not ours.

Willingness to continue a long time in prayer for something is one way we can show we mean business. Haven't you occasionally asked for something, waited awhile, and then quit asking? If it's not worth *your* while, why should it be worth *His?*

Like Daniel's, our waiting may be because of the strength of the opposition. "Because of his (the enemy's) strength will I wait upon thee: for God is my Defence."[3]

Feeling spaced? Need reinforcement? "They that wait upon the Lord shall *renew* their strength."[4]

Maybe you've just had a brush with injustice: prejudice, patronage, preferential treatment to others? Waiting in such cases takes grit. "Don't repay evil for evil. Wait for the Lord to handle the matter."[5] He can handle:

— the person who riles you or hurts your feelings
— the girl (*girl!*) who takes your job
— the guy who takes your girl
— the person who grabs the credit for *your* good work
— the one who cheats and ends up with a higher rating.

Book-balancing is God's province, not ours.

A bit of motive inspection might be overdue. *Why* do you want this thing you're waiting for?

Why? I think it's a good thing.

[3] Ps. 59:9, KJV.
[4] Isa. 40:31.
[5] Prov. 20:22.

If that's really so, you'll get it.

Who says?

God says. "No good thing will He withhold from those who walk along His paths." He does *not* say tomorrow. However, if it's too long arriving, you might want to recheck whether you're on *His* path or whether it's as good as you thought.

Is His glory a consideration?

I don't think I make the connection. I'm interested in practical things: How long I wait for a job — any job. I'm hurting financially. My car payment's overdue. My education's at stake. Yes, I want God's glory but — I don't follow.

The Bible says, "Do everything for the glory of God, even your eating and drinking."[6] And the Bible is never unrealistic. The things we do, and especially the *way* we do them, have something to do with bringing glory to God. "God's glory is man made in his image."[7] Your *attitude* as you wait can be more important than the thing for which you wait. God never takes His eyes off you, and He will not leave you stranded.

It's also possible that your waiting may involve other people known or unknown to you. Perhaps God is waiting for them in some way. My dad was the victim of cerebral hardening of the arteries at quite a young age. After a few months of violent irrationality, he settled into a near-vegetable existence. There was no cure — not even a palliative. As month after month and then a year and a second and finally a third dragged by, I pled with the Lord: "*Why?* This man has been a faithful servant of Yours." (As if God had for-

---

[6] 1 Cor. 10:31.
[7] 1 Cor. 11:7.

gotten!) I did not realize what it meant for my mother, whose mental health was fragile. The prognosis was that dad could go on for years, but she kept hoping that science would come up with some cure, some wonder drug. Finally one day she said, "It's all right. I've accepted the fact dad can't recover. I've given him over to the Lord." In two week's time pneumonia took dad into the Lord's presence. I was "ready." I'm sure dad was. But mother wasn't, and God waited until she was.

"Let not them that wait on thee . . . be ashamed for *my* sake."[8] If we run ahead of God, will this damage another? Will our impetuosity spoil something?

Waiting can be a two-way street. You're tired of waiting for God? *He* may be waiting for *you.* He waits for us to deal with:

Unconfessed sin. This can dam the flow of God's blessing. Some of today's clinical psychologists are now saying that actual moral guilt, unconfessed and un-expiated, is at the root of a great deal of mental illness, psychosis, and neurosis. Besides the primary need for us to confess our sins to the Lord, we often need to confess to the people involved in our guilty behavior and perhaps to others close to us. In this way we become free, known for who we really *are.* James, anticipating today's psychology by nearly 2000 years, wrote, "Confess your faults one to another."[9] This requires wisdom, of course. The extreme of confessing and re-confessing everything to everybody can be destructive.

Self-sufficiency. Are you getting in God's way? How can He act in your life if you insist on being the captain of your own fate?

Personality problems. Could the block be your temper, your aggressiveness, your selfishness? Have you dealt with these hangups or are you blaming God?

---

[8] Ps. 69:6, KJV.
[9] James 5:16, KJV.

Perhaps you're not sure what your problem really is, and the Holy Spirit has to point it out and then show you how to deal with it. For this, He often uses the help of wise friends.

Wrong Attitudes. To others or to yourself. Self-hate can clog the works and lead to people-hating.

How do you deal with self-hate?

A book could be written on just that. It's often rooted far back in childhood, in a sense of unworthiness fostered by early authority figures. It involves not accepting God's forgiveness and your value to Him. Do you really believe God when He says, "Neither death nor life, neither messenger of Heaven nor monarch of earth, neither what happens today nor what may happen tomorrow, neither a power from on high nor a power from below, nor anything else in God's whole world has any power to separate us from the love of God in Christ Jesus our Lord!"?[10] On a practical level, dealing with negative attitudes toward those authority figures and asking forgiveness for *your* wrong attitudes and actions will do a lot toward lifting the dark sense of worthlessness. Work of some kind, done well, helps make one feel more worthy. Even small accomplishments pulled off successfully bolster the faltering ego. One good friendship to which you give yourself is invaluable. All these things can contribute to a feeling of self-worth.

You don't feel loved or wanted? Ask God to take you to *one* person who needs *your* love, needs what you have to give. Giving love is one of the greatest ways to get love in return, but remember — it may take a lot of planting and watering, much nurturing and propping-up before this plant will bring in returns.

---

[10] Rom. 8:38, 39, Phillips.

Love is a slow-grower. Waiting again. The Christian "graces" of forgiveness, compassion, and love come from the Holy Spirit. We can't manufacture them.

Reminding ourselves of God's faithfulness in the past can be encouraging.

One of the worst things that could happen to us would be for God to "give in" and let us have our own way. The Israelis tried this. They began with a craving. This made them doubt God, and "he gave them their demands, but sent them leanness in their souls."[11]

You *must* have this thing? Careful — God just might give it to you.

It's hard to know just how to handle waiting.

Isn't it! God can give you special fellowship with Himself *as* you wait, though — a deepening trust, a closer friendship. *Now* is the only time we have to show Him our faith. When we are with Him, the days of trusting will be over. Never again, as far as I know, will we have the opportunity to show Him we trust Him.

Andrew Murray, a man of God with timeless insights into the Christian life, had some compelling thoughts on waiting. Among them: The children of Israel

> could not rise beyond their past experience or their own thought of what was possible. . . . Do let us beware of limiting the Holy One of Israel in our very prayers. Let us believe that the very promises of God we plead have a divine meaning, infinitely beyond our thoughts of them. Let us believe that His fulfillment of them can be . . . beyond our largest grasp of thought. And let us therefore cultivate the habit of waiting on God not only for what we think we need but for all His grace and power are ready to do for us. In every

---

60   [11] Ps. 106:15.

true prayer there are two hearts in exercise. The one is your heart, with its little dark human thoughts of what you need and God can do. The other is God's great heart with its infinite, its divine purposes of blessing. . . . Wait for God to do for you more than you can ask or think.

Murray thought we could hold back blessing by having our own thoughts about what God will do and thus fail to wait on

> the God of Glory according to the riches of His glory to do what has not entered the heart of man to conceive. Learn to worship God as the God who does wonders, who wishes to prove *in you* that He can do something supernatural and divine. Bow before Him, wait upon Him until your soul realizes that you are in the hands of a divine and almighty Worker. . . . Expect it to be something altogether god-like, something to be waited for in deep humility and received only by His divine power.[12]

---

[12] Andrew Murray, *Waiting on God* (Chicago: Moody Press), pp. 69-71.

6

The Name of the Game

Most of you play the dating game. Have you done much thinking about it?

Thinking? I haven't associated the two very much.

That in itself says a lot. I'd like to suggest that you men take a long look at the dating mores of your times and towns and measure them against the Christian ethic.

Perhaps you just follow the general patterns of your social set with no thought about why you do.

Questions that come up: Should there be any difference between a Christian and a non-Christian man's attitude toward dating? How honest is your attitude toward dating? Are you a totally different man on a date than when you're with a group of Christians? Do you treat women as people valued by Christ? If your dating etiquette is no different from most of your fraternity brothers, if for you one plus one always equals sex, you're flying on the wrong beam.

In many places the one-to-one ratio is the only sort of man-woman social practice expected — a sort of tribal dance. It's often the prelude to the *big proposition*. But if you're trying to live your life as God's man, you won't be doing the "in" things just because they're in.

How about creative dating?

How's that again?

You can infuse some new ideas into the social scene where you are. You've all been through the stiff, first-date horrors: Having never spent ten minutes in each other's company before, early on you and the girl may run aground conversationally. A clinch is often easier than getting off the sandbar.

Your alternative?

Group activity is one good way to get to know girls with the pressure off. Get some men together and contact some girls for action dates: swimming, skiing, skating, hill-climbing. Or go out together for some spectator sport. This way you could keep your dating a bit more selective. From the group of girls, pick one who really interests you. If you feel you have enough in common and will enjoy each other's company for a whole evening, ask her out.

Even young men can get into ruts. Do you *always* do the same thing on Saturday nights? Do you go only to movies and ball games? Is your conversation totally I-catching? How about all that leadership and daring originality of yours?

What about a project of some sort that interests you both? It doesn't have to be complicated or long-term. It could be something as simple as making taffy or cookies, as sophisticated as preparing a gourmet meal. Don't yell till you've tried it! You enjoy eating good things; you might be surprised at how much fun it is to create them.

If you've taken Susie out on three bicycle jaunts in a row, how about making the next date an occasion? Girls love a chance to dress up once in awhile.

If it is an occasion, what about *your* appearance? I know customs change and dress is often a matter of group or geographical orientation. I also realize that this is an age of studied casualness even though the much-prated individuality is conspicuous by not being there. Your decision about what you wear often rests on what pair of jeans you can *find*. However, there *are* occasions when your girl will appear in a long skirt with her hair up (Who knows? Maybe even earrings!). She will be less than enchanted if you come charging up to her door looking as if you were ready to help with the haying.

The occasion idea is out. I don't have money for that sort of thing.

If you don't, you don't. But be careful that you're not rationalizing. A girl does notice if you hand her the Poor Richard line and then sees you out downing pizzas with the boys. Or sees your record collection expanding rapidly while you chisel free meals at her apartment. I think you'll find most girls quite willing to do cheap, even no-cost things much of the time if you'll just occasionally treat her to something special.

Which brings up the subject of *using* girls. Maybe your conscience is quite clear about using them as sex objects (or maybe it isn't). What about rushing the girl with the biggest car or the one whose family has that beautiful swimming pool?

I think you may have just hit a nerve. The girl I date does have a Mercedes-Benz. But I've told her over and over that I'm not involved. We're just friends.

Her idea or yours?

She says it's O.K. She likes to be with me, likes to have me take her out. She knits me sweaters and socks and calls me up a lot. She's a great girl.

You think she feels "just friends"?

Maybe not, but — what's a guy to do?

There *is* that beautiful slinky car, yes?

There is, but I really have told her —

I've met men who feel it's O.K. to take a girl to bed with them as long as they are "honest": "You do know I don't really mean anything by this? I'm not committing myself." Could it be your conduct fits under a comparable heading? On a slightly less serious scale? *You* may feel quite uninvolved emotionally, but I don't think this absolves you of your responsibility. Women tend to be eternal optimists; if she loves you, she'll go on hoping that one day you'll switch her from the "friendly" file to the "girl I love" department. Now, if *she* agrees it's all brother-sisterhood, fine. Enjoy a good friendship. But don't be surprised if one day there comes a loud explosion — and it could be you.

You don't seem very optimistic about platonic friendships.

They're certainly not impossible, but you should recognize them as a calculated risk.

If you decide to take in a flick on a date, please do a little research. I don't have to tell you that movies for sheer entertainment are almost in the dodo category, and it might be well to know ahead of time just what sort of evening this may turn out to be. Your date may be a girl who reacts badly to violence, for instance. The tolerance level for that sort of thing varies a lot from person to person. *You* may thoroughly enjoy it, but she may play and replay those scenes in her mind for weeks and have nightmares. Some films are better seen with other men. (Consideration department: Have you ever asked yourself *why* you get such a charge out of violence? Transference? Wish-fulfillment? Whatever it is, it might merit a little sober thinking. "He [the Lord] hates those loving violence.")[1]

If it's a film that shows explicit sex scenes or if perversion is its theme, you might both want to talk about your motives in seeing it. Is it because "everyone" says it's great (You're a sheep, maybe?), the *Time* review says it's a "must," or do you really respect the producer and feel this will make a valuable commentary on some angle of today's thinking? I am not saying see only Mary Poppins-type films. I *am* saying that each of us needs to think carefully before we see many of today's films. Our motives can come from the prurience that lies just below the surface in all of us. Seeing a controversial film with other Christians and discussing it before and after can be good.

Have you thought about asking the Lord to guard your subconscious? Does that sound weird? A large part of what goes on in the human mind is on the unconscious level, a sort of data processing station

[1] Ps. 11:5.

tending to have more control over our behavior than our conscious mind. Every thought that passes through our conscious mind is registered indelibly on our subconscious mind.

We can't control our subconscious mind!

No, but a lot of what goes down there sifts through the permissive grid of our consciousness. We can't control everything, but we need to be careful what we choose to store in our impression attics.

Whether to go to certain kinds of social events or not, whether to go only to Christian events or to include non-Christian scenes is something I think no one can give you rules for. For me, this is involved in "the just shall live by *faith.*" Are you willing to carefully consider each individual occasion? What might be good for you and permissible in your Father's sight one week might not be the thing He wants you to attend another week. Various things could affect your decision: your present communication with the Lord (strong or weak?); your own particular weaknesses (If alcohol or hash is your vulnerable area, why stick your neck out?). Can you remain strong in the Lord at this scene or are you apt to be inundated? On Tuesday there may be a better way to spend your time than on something that was quite O.K. last Friday. You do not have an unyielding Father who never wants you to have fun. And I think His children can add immeasurably to their enjoyment of fun things if they feel He is smiling with them. "The Lord . . . hath pleasure in the prosperity of his servant."[2] Some people are able to go to very unlikely places and remain detached and compassionate, but the majority of us tend

---

[2] Ps. 35:27, KJV.

to be social chameleons and take on the color of our environment.

In a way, you know, it's lots *easier* to have rules: "Never do this, Never go there. . . ." But it can make us insensitive to people and situations and can undermine our existential walk with the Lord.

Some of you date a girl a few times and get an acute case of the "big cattleman" syndrome. You eyeball a girl and say to yourself: "That one is *mine*." You all but rope, tie, and brand the girl. Huge scenes if she dates someone else. Better wait till you are ready to commit yourself to one woman and it's a mutual thing.

Another thing I find the ladies distinctly do *not* go for is swapping bets on prospects: "I'll take Josephine out if you can wangle a date with Anne." Not good sportsmanship, gentlemen.

Girls find some of you paranoid about being pursued. Admittedly, there are a few female lioness types around, but surely they're in the minority? Don't start running before you see the whites of their claws.

One thing I get burned about: Why is it always the guy who has to spend the money?

It depends, doesn't it, on the current social standards of your particular college or business set? This should be something you discuss in the group. You and your girl can reach a clear understanding. Some couples work out a Dutch-treat arrangement satisfactorily; some girls wouldn't pay for a coke. You'd better survey the situation, but *do* communicate.

By the way, when you *do* pay, be careful you don't project the feeling that taking the girl out a time or two *entitles* you to something. Many of you don't think this way, but some do. You can make a girl feel 68 that if she doesn't want to kiss you good-night, she's not giving you value for your money. A few even act as if a dinner entitles them to bedroom privileges.

Girls still like the small attentions. Times and customs change here too, but on the whole the basic nature of the species does not. The lady will enjoy being treated as someone special — having courtesy shown her, even doors opened or chairs held (though *that* may so startle her the first time it might take her a little while to recover). Small gifts will bring her pleasure.

Gifts aren't in my budget.

Small gifts. Something you make could be very meaningful to her.

What do you look for in girls you date? What are your requirements?

Number One: Appearance. I like to feel proud to be seen with any woman I squire around.

Not commenting for the moment on your priorities, may I ask what *kind* of appearance?

Great figure, right clothes for the right place, oh — and a nice face, good eyes, and good legs.

In a word, sexy.

Right on.

Realizing I may sound just a shade grandmotherly: Have you ever wondered why your requirements are so physically oriented? Have you considered that the way your thinking is centered is given away even in   69 the way you *look* a girl over? What, exactly, is on your mind?

I'm certainly not out to MARRY the girl the first time we go out together.

I hope not. What *are* you out for?

Like the man said: Fun, a good time. "Double your pleasure, double your fun —"

There's nothing wrong in hoping a girl will be easy on the eyes, but what about priorities? Also, what is it you want her to find irresistible in *you*? Is it those muscles, that great suntan you picked up at Laguna Beach, your high-powered animal magnetism?

Sure don't mind her noticing.

No, I suppose not. But in the long run?

I want her to care about ME — as I am, with or without suntan. I want her to value me as a person.

Good. But she's a person too.

Let me quote from a letter from a friend — a 6-foot-4-inch Christian athlete. In discussing the difference between *femininity* and *sexiness* he said, "When I have my head on right — which may take a few moments initially — I'll long for the former. In this kind of girl there seems to be a sureness of the value of 'He that is faithful in that which is least is faithful also in much . . . ,' and who among us wants anything more than a faithful wife?"

I think I might like this guy. But we haven't been talking about wives yet.

Shouldn't every girl be considered as a human being first? Shouldn't even a one-time-only date be a sharing experience, not just something *you* are going to feel good about? Dates involve mutual development. It's not unrealistic to think you each can be a little better, stronger, happier at the end of an evening together.

I guess I haven't taken it that seriously.

The danger in too much appearance-orientation is that it can easily become sex-orientation. Your evening out could turn into an anatomy course in braille, after which it's not easy to revert to discussing next week's Bible study.

Have you ever considered this girl you're taking out as your sister in Christ?

My SISTER!

She really is, you see. That's not a concept; it's a reality.

But look here. You can't mean —

We always seem to put the emphasis on the negative aspects. What about the *positive* side? How *does* a man treat his sister?

I don't have any.

How do you think you would treat a much-loved sister if you did have one?

Let's see. I'd enjoy her as a person: her mind, her personality. I'd be interested in her ideas on things. I'd feel very protective of her. In fact, I'd break any man's neck that so much as — mm. I see what you're getting at.

Your date is *somebody's* sister; if not, you're still to consider her as a valuable human being.

I hope you're not saying don't date — just admire from a distance?

Hardly. But I am suggesting you take a long look at girls as *real people;* that you consider the fact that God, whom you have taken as Lord of your life, has cast you in the role of protector and leader. The whole upside-down role reversal has brought about some very upside-down morality.

What about personality, character, communication? If you're even mildly intellectual, a whole evening spent with a lady who isn't will lead to either boredom or you know what else. Or if you're a member of the tennis set and she's a bookworm, a good time may not be had by all.

Girls seem to EXPECT certain behavior from men. I don't want my dates thinking I'm not a man — that I'm gay.

Have the courage to be who you are.

Planning a date's not a bad idea. Consider something the girl will find interesting. Be realistic about the kind of evening that's going to set your hormones doing a war dance. "Let's just drive around" is the opening line for the melodrama whose curtain comes down on the backseat. I must say I find your generation is more open and honest in facing this whole problem than mine was, but you still play a good many games.

72

Have you ever thought that your game playing may begin before you're anywhere near the girl? In your room, in the dorm, at your apartment as you get ready for a date: mood music, the after-shave lotion, the quick flashes of yourself in action? What are you setting the stage for?

If you're not careful, you can get caught up in one of the assorted games men play. A few samples:

— *You're my everything.* (What he's really saying is, "Can I borrow your convertible?")

— *I can't wait to see you, doll.* (This translates into, "I'm hot to trot.")

— *We're just friends aren't we?* (Meaning, "You'll do until someone more exciting comes along.")

— *I can't make it tonight, babe, it's exam week.* (What he means is, "There's a new tomato in the basket, and I'm going to be first in line at the market.")

Communication plays a vital part in any human association. It's a two-way street. Find out what the *girl* thinks. Girls, as many of you do know, have minds — some of them quite good ones. They enjoy having a man appreciate them. They can also come up with some good ideas about you and your interests — even your problems. Good friendships can develop between attractive Christian guys and girls who've learned to be open and honest with each other, who deal with each other as persons with interests, ideas, and talents worth learning about.

Then there is the most significant factor of all: This girl has a spiritual nature. If she is a Christian, the great river of the life in Christ runs in both of you. It is the deepest part of each of you and is there to be tapped and explored. Prayer, too, can be an integral part of the Christian dating scene.

You mean pray about who to take out?   **73**

That, yes. I think *every* phase of our lives is worth bringing to our Father. But what I am thinking about now is praying *together* — praying about where to spend your time, what to do, committing the evening to the Lord, being open and honest about the whole tricky business of sexual attraction. (Some of you tell me this doesn't work well for you. That it only makes the focus more intimate. If this happens to you, then this suggestion's not for you.)

If you tackle dating from the standpoint of the Christian ethic, you'll find yourself growing as a Christian and developing some worthwhile friendships with girls. Because of mass media and the overwhelming consensus, you will also find yourself a salmon swimming upstream. You may well be teased, jeered at, or accused of being gay. Still, if Christ is not Lord in your sports car, at the fraternity house, or in your head when you're trying to decide about going to the local hash-bash, then He's not really Lord at all, is He?

7

Great Expectations

We women are supposed to be the daydreamers, but I find that you men do a fair share of aerodynamic castle-building. As you think about your ideal girl, what's she like?

Appearance is high on the list, as we mentioned before.

Top priority?

Mmm-mmmm — I suppose not, if I get down to basics. As your correspondent in the dating chapter says: When I have my head on right, I realize that femininity tops sexiness, but my head can get twisted at some strange angles.

Have you thought about asking God to shape your ideas and ideals?

Where do MY mind and tastes come in?

They'll enter into it, you can be sure. Sometimes you men get into trouble because you have a definite mind-set toward one particular type of girl based on the unshakeable assurance that you know just what you want and just what's good for you.

I'm sure I do.

Can you really be sure? Remember, God is the one who put complex you together. He knows all your springs, wheels, and parts, movable and immovable. *Also* your hangups, forgotten childhood influences, psychological twists, environmental conditions — to name a few.

The basis for your standard could be shaky if you don't know women as well as you think you do. A gorgeous girl who says, "Oh, you great big hunk of beautiful man," may strike you as a most perceptive woman — but watch it! That kind of lady can be so well-schooled in her responses to men that those lines come out like tape from a calculating machine.

Granted that you're initially attracted by a girl's looks; but surely a man with your brains is going to search beyond looks? Aren't you interested in what a lady thinks?

Oh sure. I do steer clear of the girl who tries to dazzle me with her brains, though.

You feel threatened?

Not at all. I don't mind her knowing things I don't know. I'm quite capable of saying, "I'm not up on that subject. Fill me in." No, the girl who puts me off is the

one who either tries to snow me with her intellect or the

one who is so sure of herself that she only wants a man around for decoration.

You're not being so unrealistic as to look for one girl who has it all?

No, no. I know it's a fallen world —

But there does seem to be the temptation to go on this Diogenes hunt — not for an honest man, but for the perfect woman. Put down your lantern; the search is over. There's no such girl. One girl is never going to have everything — two hundred times in your copybook, please because you'll save yourself a lot of grief if you believe it.

You may find one person with looks and brains and charm who has *no* interest in your most absorbing interest. Or you may find a gem of a little cook who would be so fascinated with homemaking that you'd get left in the cold. Another may make you feel you're the greatest man in the world, but it is only feeding her own vanity. Marriage needs to be a working partnership.

General compatibility is important: Two great people may be all wrong together. Just because a girl is beautiful or intelligent or has a crazy sense of humor like yours or a cute little nose doesn't necessarily mean she's the girl who'll fill your needs for a lifetime.

Why not line up all the things you would like your girl to have and then sort them out on a priority basis? Please pray, because the Holy Spirit can guide your mind to things most important for *you,* even things you may not have considered before. You think you'd like a girl who'd burn incense at your shrine, have your pipe and slippers ready at night, and hang on your your every word?

Sounds great for my insecurities.

Does it? The Lord may show you that you need a girl who will love you truly but will see you realistically, who will recognize your weaknesses and help you grow. Not as *comfortable,* maybe, but in the long run you'll achieve greater stature with the second girl than with the first.

It's important to find someone you can *be yourself* with — someone who appreciates the real you.

There are some girls who know me very well, but I never think of them as anything but friends.

I don't know anything about these particular girls, but believe me, in day after day togetherness, married life can be a lot smoother with a woman who has no illusions about you and loves you anyway. A wonderful bedmate might bore you right round the bend any other time. Someone with whom you can share your ideas, who understands and loves you as *you are* will never (Well, hardly ever!) bore you.

But suppose there's NO physical attraction?

Since God is the initiator of coupleness, He's not apt to ask you to marry a girl for whom you feel only brotherly affection. So drop *that* worry into the circular file.

Do you look at a girl, drop her card into your private mind-computer, and, if the results don't fit your pre-set specifications, burn the card? Remember, two can play at that game: Girls have their own rating system.

78   **Suppose I'm taking a Christian girl out. I like her, but**

I'm not serious at all. How does what you're saying fit here?

I'd suggest praying about your attitude toward her and asking to be made sensitive to her feelings toward you. Often (not always) girls are more marriage-minded than men. Try to notice if she is getting involved, and rather than sunning in the warmth of her response to you, try to protect her from getting hurt.

Another thing: Don't try to make any girl over into something she's not. You're defensive, rightly so, about girls who want to remodel you. Don't try to revamp girls to your mind-model. God has made us unique. He respects the differences He's built in. Shouldn't we?

On the other hand, you may find a girl who is *too* willing to adapt.

How's that?

She might spend lots of time and effort attempting to be the girl you expect her to be, and nothing comes of your relationship. Then who is she for the next man in her life? (Admittedly, this would be a girl not very sure of who she is, but there are lots of them around.)

Don't ever demand perfection in any girl you meet, and never, *never* in yourself. Dr. Francis Schaeffer of L'Abri Fellowship in Switzerland points out that in the long run utopian demands are always cruel.

There is much potential pain and psychological injury in man-woman involvements; even one bad experience can bring destructive tendencies to the surface like pond scum. A man finds himself tearing a girl down so his own weaknesses won't show up. Or running another man down in an effort to reinforce his own ego. A critical attitude aligns us with the wrong side: It's Satan who is "the accuser of the brethren" — sistern too. Paul Tournier, the Swiss psychiatrist, holds that criticism invariably raises such a storm of inner self-justification in the one criticized that the quiet voice of God can't get through.

If this happens to be a problem of yours, ask yourself *why* you are being so destructive. Talking it over with some sympathetic friend could help you be objective. Bitterness pulls in others like the center of a whirlpool. Your bitterness can contaminate all around you.

Then there's the dependency syndrome: Are you spending more and more time with some girl because you are finding it comfortable to lean on her? Or if you're playing big he-man to her l'il ole clingin' vine you may find yourself overgrown. While she may think you have everything, you know jolly well you have not. The more she invests total dependency in you, the more *in*adequate you're going to feel and the less you'll dare to admit those inadequacies. Eventually you'll feel schiz, and one day you may just move on. In which case, there will be damage on both sides.

It's important for Christians to consider whether we are more interested in what we *get* from any association than what we give to it.

Perhaps you should ask yourself if you see everything about a girl in direct relation to *you: your* pride in her, *your* success, *your* career, the impression *you* make.

Ouch! My toes are hurting.

In relating to women — a sister, the girl you made mud pies with, or the most exciting girl in the world — your ideal (*ideal,* I'm saying) should be giving, not getting.

Not easy. And it isn't where most of my friends' heads are at.

The first century Christians must have had similar problems. "Don't let the world around you squeeze you into its own mould,"[1] Paul wrote and Jesus spoke about giving being better than getting.

We need to be honest with ourselves about motives. Our twistedness is such that even in giving we are only too capable of giving to buy response. The canoe can tip in either direction; 100 percent pure motives just aren't part of this fallen world.

Is your built-in computer automatically clicking off age differences?

Don't they count?

Maybe not as much as our society has made them. They shouldn't be *the* controlling factor, should they? One can generalize and say that too much difference in age may not be good, or that it's usually "better" for the man to be older than the girl, but most of us know outstanding exceptions to both rules. To dodge a friendship on the basis of age difference could cut you off from something good.

And how about looking for a girl you can pray with?

Out loud?

It's not easy to share prayer in a silent way. Praying about mutual concerns in an open, informal way can add a new dimension to the friendship. If you can do this easily — fine. If you can't now — relax. There may come a day when you'll want to.

You have great expectations for your ideal girl. That's as it should be. Just be sure:

---

[1] Rom. 12:2, Phillips.

— that you are open-minded about the type of girl who will be "right" for you;

— that you are realistic about what you are looking for, keeping in mind which traits are most important and remembering that all the goodies you like will never come in one package;

— that you face reality — you're relating to a flesh and blood woman, finite, marred by the Fall as you are, not some goddess-girl from outer space;

— that, most important of all, you don't live a layered Christianity. Include God in all this from the outset. Many bad experiences would never happen if we'd started praying a lot earlier. Talk to God about your expectations, trying to be very open with Him. Ask Him to keep you clear-headed, to show you your weaknesses, and to help you in that area in which we are all so vulnerable — self-deception.

8

Your Rating for Mating

Having considered your expectations, what about *you?* Are you the kind of man this paragon is going to be attracted to?

You ask some of the most uncomfortable questions! How do I know?

Your attraction for her will be based on many things, ranging from your own appearance to your emotional maturity.

How would you define emotional maturity?

A partial definition would be the ability to *give* rather than demand love and its lesser variants: attention and affection. Maurice Wagner of the Narramore Clinic in California thinks that we can divide emotional maturity into four stages which can be equated with four stages in child development.

You'll have to clue me.

A tiny baby has needs. He yells; he gets. It's that simple. When an adult *demands* things just because he wants them, when his is a "gimme" orientation, that person's emotional maturity could be rated as infantile. Mind you, we all can and do regress to this first stage from time to time.

A child's life normally develops from this stage to the second one where he finds he can manipulate to get what he wants. He learns how to be consciously charming, or he tries the "Mommy, I'm thirsty" routine at bedtime.

Ah, yes. I have known some great manipulators in my time.

You know the scene then: Joe muscles in on Ray's territory with his girl friend; Harry always "happens" to arrive at Judy's apartment at dinner time.

Mastery's the key word in stage two. We manipulate to master the person, the group, the situation. (Big business thrives on stage two — it's the Madison Avenue creed. Make people want what they don't need, buy what they can't afford. The methods range from the blatant to the subliminal.) There are, the theory runs, the controlled and the controllers and the smartest manipulator gets the kewpie doll.

In our private lives many of us stay in stage two a great deal of the time. Sometimes our own motives are too subtle for us to be fully aware of them. Take the girl who's always dropping by with a problem. By making people feel sorry for her and getting them involved with her problem-oriented thinking, she thinks she's being helped. What she's really doing is "managing" people to get their time and affection.

84

Or the person with frequent depressive moods. He may feel that's "his nature," but he uses these moods to force people to give him the attention he craves.

There is the socially gauche manipulator. He meets a newly engaged couple en route to the theater. Politely (but only politely) they suggest he join them. They need him not at all. He protests, "No, No. I couldn't possibly. Good of you but — well — (pause) do you really want me? (second pause) Of course I'd *love* to, it's my favorite play. O.K. you twisted my arm." And off he goes exactly as he planned.

One of the least tolerable forms of manipulation is in "Christian finances." We all know God leads some to depend on Him to provide their material needs. They work, and work hard, sans salary or "visible means of support" in some sort of "full-time service" or missionary effort. If this life, however, is going to be by faith, let's have it faith in the Lord not "faith and postage stamps." The prayer letter which suggests very gently that "I'm down to my last cent, don't know how I'm going to meet those big dental bills coming up but. . . . Of course, the Lord does take care of His own. . . ." And out go 2000 copies of said prayer letter. I think this is another form of manipulation. "I want the Lord to take care of me, but I'd better help Him out," seems to equal, "I must be in control."

And stage three?

This is the tit-for-tat mentality. For instance, a man dates a girl, phones her, takes her presents. *But,* in return he wants — well, *what* he wants will vary according to his personality, his mores, his spiritual development. But if he's on the third level he'll want *something,* if it's only X amount of time. Many of us spend much time in stage three. Rarely can we break the pattern on our own.

The ultimate in maturity, stage four, is giving simply because there is a need. Now our ego needs support from *some* source. If we rely on God, not on our friends, to support it (that is, if we live in conscious awareness of His acceptance of us as His own children), we become more free to give without insisting on "value received." It means allowing God to be to us all He wants to be. In the matter of giving (money, time, friendship) it also means sifting our motives through the sieve of His viewpoint. In the man-woman relationship it requires special wisdom to know how to give in this way without getting emotionally trapped oneself or hurting someone else.

Of course no one stays neatly compartmentalized in any one stage. In a day, in an hour, even, we can shift in and out of all four.

This is going to take some thinking about.

Going on with your qualifications: What about personal leadership? How do you rate there?

Keep talking.

What kind of leadership do you want to give your girl friend, perhaps later your wife and children?

Certainly moral and ethical leadership, a loving kind of leadership that would strengthen their own growth with the Lord.

Fine. Leadership presupposes knowledge. Knowledge of God's character (among other things), knowledge of the Bible, and most certainly in-depth, experiential knowledge of God Himself. In order to strengthen someone else's closeness with God, your own must be a daily challenge to them. Do you have a genuine friendship with the Lord, or are you following some formula set by a group, organization, or church? Are you shaping your relationship with God on that of your friends? God has made you different from them; your relationship with Him will be different. Do you *enjoy* your friendship with the Lord? Do you believe He loves you as you are? Do you spend time on your own learning what He is like? These are some of the questions involved.

In your interaction with others your attitude will count. People will follow what they see externally. No matter how well you speak, no matter how much you enjoy your quiet times, the way you live your life is what speaks loudly — both to other Christians and to non-Christians. There are no externals if there are no roots, but roots are not what we see. Fruit and flowers are what we see. Or, to change the metaphor: the cutting edge of your leadership can be blunted by your life style. Today's Christian leadership is in danger of so closely following the pattern of "bigger is better" that there is nothing in its way of life that challenges. We need to ask ourselves what it is that shapes our attitudes, what sets the pace for us. *Why* do we have the type of home we have? *Why* do we go the pace we do? Is there some good reason behind our spending? Do we exhibit the *beauty* and freedom inherent in the Christian way of life? What is it that makes our life style a worthy blueprint for anyone else?

Discipline is involved in Christian leadership. One of the New Testament requirements for men who are Christian leaders is the discipline of their own children. This is future tense for some of you right now, though there are those of you with broken marriages who still have responsibility for your children. "If you refuse to discipline your son, it proves you don't love him."[1]

---

[1] Prov. 13:24.

Are you establishing *now* the basis on which such discipline will rest? How's your score with any children you presently have responsibility for: children at your church, your math pupils, your kid brothers and sisters, or those of your friends? It takes sensitivity not to go overboard and exceed your limits, but God seems to give us learning situations for future responsibilities.

Although they are basically specifications for church leadership, the lists Paul wrote young Timothy and Titus indicate some things God looks for in His leaders. Such things as self-control, discretion, self-discipline, moderation, non-violence, non-materialism, blamelessness. . . .

I'm out!

The list could be overwhelming were it not for the fact that God never asks us to live *any* part of the Christian life in our own strength. It's *His* power that's available to us. We say this phrase with ease, don't we? It becomes practically a cliché. But what *about* His power? Think of tornados, tidal waves, the awesomeness of the hydrogen bomb — or even the great force in a tree root that can force its way through concrete and undermine buildings. "These are some of the minor things he does, merely a whisper of his power."[2]

The significant people in your life have every right to expect dependability from you. In your home you will be responsible for major decisions. Do today's friends find you dependable? Dependability is a trait learned through accepting responsibility. Don't be discouraged if to date you have not managed to be very dependable. Honestly try to grow in this area; tackle

[2] Job 26:14.

even the small responsibilities that come your way and ask God to change you where you need changing. That may sound easy; actually it's a prayer that takes much courage. But He will do it if you want Him to.

And — whatever happened to decisiveness? The girls I talk with often grumble that today's men don't seem decisive.

I don't like to be domineering.

Not the same thing, is it? Most women like a man to know what he's doing, even in casual situations. If you're taking a girl out to dinner, know where you're going. Don't diddle the evening away doing the "Where do *you* want to go?" routine.

But I like to give a girl a choice.

Then by all means let her choose, but give her a range of choices within your budget. Otherwise you'll have only yourself to blame if she leads you to the most expensive restaurant in town.

Gini, there are ten girls on my list right now who would have my head on a cheap tin tray if I tried to be the big decision-maker all the time.

Not *all* the time. And you're not the decision-maker for *ten* girls (nor will you ever be unless you come up with nine daughters). Hackles down, please. What we're considering is the fact that you may be in training for the position of husband and father. Don't expect to waffle around in your present man-woman associations and then, when rings are exchanged, suddenly emerge as "heap big Indian." The ability to handle   89 major decisions is the product of making small ones well.

Some of you, of course, may need to err in the other direction. A girl may admire a man who knows where he's going and who makes her feel cared for, but that doesn't mean she'll go for the cave man act.

It comes back to love, doesn't it? Christian love expressed in practical situations. Think about the man-woman association as a sharing experience. In each individual case there can be things for you to learn from the girl, things she can learn from you. With each girl there should be something you can give her that will make her a richer person: your own individual experience, understanding, viewpoints. With any girl you will ever date there can be some positive thing that will enrich your life or contribute to growth.

Summing it up: How free a person are you? Are you satisfied with who you are or is there some spade work to be done? You don't have to remain where you are. If you're not satisfied with your qualifications, you can change. There's all that power available. The Christian life is a life of new beginnings. Do you believe it? *Live it!!*

9

Does Your Biology Fit Your Theology?

The subject of sex has sometimes been unrealistically handled by evangelical Christians. We have divided our attitudes between Victorian hush-hush and an incredible romantic escapism. We tend to be five to eight years behind where the action is, in some cases — fifty. Many of you young Christians have been brought up in an atmosphere of veiled hostility to the subject of sex, a hostility based on a frightened refusal to cope with what is happening in the whole Western world. In some quarters this is made more unrealistic by an insistance on remaining in the world of Rock Hudson-Doris Day, of *Sound of Music* and *My Fair Lady*.

While we reject the tendency to treat sex as an uninhibited national pastime with no rules and a total wipe-out of responsibility, we may need to ask ourselves what shapes *our* attitudes. Where are *we* getting our ideals? Are we evading the ugly facts of the permissive society by escaping into a cotton-candy world where boy-meets-girl, birds sing, music plays, and they live happily ever after? Then what will be our solutions when things don't work out in real life the way they're "supposed to"?

What *does* shape your attitude to sex and couple-ness? Maybe you are influenced more than you know by figures like Mick and Bianca Jagger. Or if it's not romantic escapism in a new guise, is it Masters and Johnson with their icy clinical reports, Fromm's *Art of Loving*, or the proliferating encounter groups? Are we Christians unconsciously governed by the law of the "norm," accepting unanalytically the majority view-point, à la Kinsey and Co.?

Man *is* what God has made him, whether or not he subscribes to this fact. He is a moral being, and body and psyche are controlled by God's laws irrespective of his belief in them. Whatever his credo, there will always be something within a human being that is painfully destroyed if he goes against who he is. One of Britain's gifted young poets, Steve Turner, sums it up:

> My love
>> she said
>> that when all's
>> considered
>> we're only
>> machines.
> I chained
>> her to my
>> bedroom wall
>> for future use
>> and she cried.[1]

This is certainly no plea to return to the Victorian Era of antimacassars and embarrassed sexual hypocrisy.

---

[1] Steve Turner, "The Conclusion," from *Tonight We Will Fake Love* (London: Charisma Books, 1974).

It is good to be able to discuss sex openly, to see it as God-given, to try to learn the right way to deal with it.

One of the reasons the "Christian ethic" has been laughed at is because what has gone by that name has concentrated almost exclusively on thou-shalt-nots. It's important to realize that we have a *positive* viewpoint, and because it considers man as God's creation, it's both universal and timeless. In a world rapidly discovering the law of diminishing returns in the sexual area, we need not be on the defensive. We have a strong alternative that is also beautiful.

The biblical view of sex is that it is an integral part of a permanent relationship, a beautiful and deeply personal matter involving two people committed to one another. Since God created human beings to live this way, they will function best and be most fulfilled if they follow His design. Our view, of course, is that they are not programmed to do this; they may choose. However, since this is the Designer's standard, any attempt to break with it is going to be harmful to the individuals involved.

It's interesting that the farther religions get from what we Christians believe to be revealed truth, the more degrading and impersonal their sex practices become. One need only cite India or our own post-Christian culture. The farther it has come from belief in the Judaeo-Christian God, the greater the promiscuity, perversion, and degradation of man as a significant being. The view of man as the product of a fortuitous combination of energy particles has had its effect on sexual mores. And why not? After all, if man is only a machine without personal value, computerized by the DNA templet to a predetermined existence, why *not* throw caution overboard? Who's to set limits? What's to keep us from doing anything we please with anyone?

One of the many reasons to jealously guard the

validity of the first chapters of Genesis is that here we have the first statement about man and woman and the significance of their togetherness. One man and one woman together were created to be Man in the first instance, and together they were made in God's image. "They two shall be one flesh" was said of this first couple. Christ endorsed the Genesis statement that a man is to leave father and mother for his partner and cleave to her. He spoke of this as being "from the beginning," authenticating both God's view of man and woman and the Genesis view of creation. We cannot reject either without impugning both Jesus' veracity and the Bible's infallibility. We also jettison the Bible's high view of man.

The whole idea of the physical union expressing a true oneness accompanied by a permanent commitment is being discarded as absurd and unnecessary. Our technology has invaded the sexual arena with chilly voiced authority. The Masters and Johnson approach has taken an act that involves the meshing of two significant beings in life's most intimate involvement and put it under the white light of clinical observation complete with TV cameras and detached observers in white coats. Men and women have come to view their sex lives in much the same way as they view their car when it gives them trouble: run it into the garage, put it up on the rack, and have a mechanic find out why it doesn't work. They consider their sex life of towering importance (which it is) but something that is separated from other areas of themselves: personality, emotion, commitment, spiritual values (which it is not).

You don't think there's a place for sex counseling?

The sex counselor may have helped some of his
94 patients understand the workings of their sexual

natures, but even establishing sexual harmony between partners may well overlook much deeper problems concerned with relating to one another as human beings. "Practicing" with a surrogate is certainly divorcing sex from its God-given place in the total fabric of wholeness between one human being and his chosen mate.

The biblical sexual ideal is permeated with love. It recognizes sex for the great life force it is and shows God's outlet for it to be the permanent commitment of marriage, which allows for *time* in developing sexual harmony.

Today's "emancipated" person hoots at this. Sex is funny, clever, necessary, natural, a kick, and harmless. It is harmful to abstain. It used to be harmful just for the men; now women are included in the club. (Think of the millions of women who had the misfortune of living their whole lives in a nonpermissive society!)

Now if our statistics showed that today there are fewer women with nervous breakdowns, fewer who become alcoholics or drug addicts, fewer who commit suicide, we might say, *"Look!* The liberated female! She has come into her own, and there she stands: a fulfilled and free person." The facts are in direct contradiction to this.

But this is a book for men. Are men harmed by promiscuity? Society has always held that it's the woman who pays, while the man can go scot free (unless he's either stupid or unlucky). Today's rakes hardly need to progress to brothels: unfortunately girls are becoming as available as dandelions on a suburban lawn.

Since I am writing mainly to Christian men who believe the Bible to be true, it should not be hard for you to accept the Bible's statements that men by no means come off unscathed in the promiscuity promenade. **95**

Speaking of brothels, Proverbs makes a surprising statement: "None of these men (who go there) will ever be the same again."[2] One thinks of psychological damage, in spite of the general nonchalance, for one cannot destroy any part of another human being's personality without also killing some part of oneself.

But professional prostitutes —

— are made in God's image. No one has the right to further debase even a prostitute.

Scripture never blinks at the fact that sin can be fun. Solomon, a man hardly naive in this sphere, said, "For the lips of a prostitute are as sweet as honey, and smooth flattery is her stock in trade (Sound contemporary?). But (cause and effect) afterwards only a bitter conscience is left to you, sharp as a double-edged sword."[3]

A lot of men I know don't seem to feel any guilt about promiscuity.

That's even sadder, isn't it? It means either a total disregard for women as people or a conscience so tough it has lost its ability to function.

Don't be dazzled by the erroneous idea that your generation is liberated. Society, even while it remains permissive, makes its own wryly contemptuous comment on its mores in the names given social centers where the avowed intent is Operation Bedtime: The Meat Rack, Body Works, Pig Place. Far from experiencing a free and joyous way of life, many of the swinging singles receive, or are hiding, deep psychological pain. One psychotherapist's analysis of the

---

[2] Prov. 2:19.
[3] Prov. 5:3, 4.

"swingles" mentality is that these people purposely anesthetize themselves so well that they are no longer aware they are in pain. They may well be afraid of close relationships — even incapable of them. Solomon lived 3000 years before the "new morality," and as far as I know his score with women has never been equaled: 700 wives and 300 concubines. As a sexual athlete he remains unchallenged, but he ended with the taste of dust in his mouth and said sadly: "One man among a thousand have I found; but a woman among all those have I not found."[4] What was the problem? Certainly not available women. It was the law of diminishing returns again. The loss of a quality relationship in such quantitative experience. "The man who commits adultery is an utter fool, for he destroys his own *soul*. Wounds and constant disgrace are his lot."[5]

We are fast becoming a society that refuses to face reality of any sort if it involves discomfort. Ads assure us that product X will alleviate physical pain immediately. The fact that pain is sometimes a necessary warning of a deeper disturbance is hardly considered. As for psychological pain: drown it, drug it, put it to bed.

Do you find yourself living on two levels: the straightforward, responsible Christian youth leader on Sunday and church nights and in between someone whose anatomy is causing a dichotomy?

What's a man to do these days?

These days? Christian sex ethics weren't any cinch in the first century either. Rome wasn't River City. Even then Paul was writing, "Remember this — the

---

[4] Eccles. 7:28, KJV.
[5] Prov. 6:32, 33.

wrong desires that come into your life aren't anything new and different. Many others have faced exactly the same problems before you." He adds: "Carefully avoid idol-worship of every kind."[6]

Idol worship? I thought we were discussing sex.

We are. Can you think of anything that comes closer to being an international religion than sex? It is top priority in millions of lives. The sex scorekeeping in the swingles complexes, the mate-swapping, the casual use of all kinds of overt sex symbols as decoration, the enormous amount of pornography, the commercialization and exploitation of the human body in ads, entertainment, etc. — what else can we call it? Even our language is so raddled with sexual allusions that one never knows when the most ordinary word may be added to the long list of words with libidinous overtones.

Pornography is older than Hugh Hefner by many centuries. Hindu temples and Pompeian walls show as advanced pornography as anything you'll pick up on the newsstands. We all have in us a nature that gravitates to that sort of thing if we allow it. (Oh, we may not admit it, or we may refine it down a little. We wouldn't think of buying porn at the neighborhood store where we're known. Dirty postcards are out, but if there's something salacious in the evening paper or *Time.* . . . No one will fault us here!) We're all fallen, and we need God's strength to keep from pandering to our fallen instincts. And common sense. For instance, walking certain streets is a little like running your finger over a razor blade to see if it can draw blood, and there *is* another route to the bank, yes?

Each man has his own threshold of tolerance in the

[6] 1 Cor. 10:13, 14.

sexual area. For some, certain films are off-limits. It isn't "chicken" not to see them; it's just good sense. For others, certain books aren't worth the price. It's intelligent to avoid situations where the pull of the body and imagination become irresistible. What you do about the Lord's values is important. Where do your loyalties lie?

God has made you a man, with all that implies. The sex drive is a force that has managed to keep the world populated since Adam and Eve, so there's no point in underestimating it. However, even the driving force that launches a rocket needs to be controlled and perfectly timed — otherwise, disaster. Correct?

But I'm not a machine.

Exactly. You're not. The Lord Himself showed us that a man can be a man, live a life world-shaking in its impact, and remain a virgin.

But He was God.

He was. But apart from sin, he was completely human.

Some of your contemporaries see the Christian sex ethic as a return to Puritanism. It antedates the Puritans by several millenniums. Nor is it an invention of the twentieth century evangelical church. Copulating with many women distorts what God intended the sex act to represent: wholeness on a human level (and something even higher that we'll discuss in the marriage chapter). Sex as a self-gratifying end is a travesty of God's design. Instead of the great culmination of love between a man and a woman, a culmination based on respect, emotional involvement, and permanence, man has twisted it into something that exists 99 per se, every man's "right." (I use the term "man" generically; woman have been cooperative distorters.)

Your contemporaries talk of freedom. No one's more a total slave than the man who gets hooked on his body's demands. The pathetic bachelor from Houston quoted in *Saturday Review*[7] ("I'm into playin' and lovin' and not givin' a damn for the rest of my life.") thinks he's finally free, but he's got himself so conditioned to performing as a sexual roadrunner that he is more of a captive than an animal in a zoo.

Promiscuity is one of the things Scripture is explicit about: "You cannot say that our physical body was made for sexual promiscuity," which is certainly what is being said today. "It was made *for God*, and God is the answer to our deepest longings."[8] "Run from sex sin. No other sin affects the body as this one does. When you sin this sin it is against your own body. Haven't you yet learned that your body is the home of the Holy Spirit God gave you, and that he lives within you? Your own body does not belong to you. For God has bought you with a great price. (And here is the positive approach.) So use every part of your body to give glory to God, because he owns it."[9]

It's hard when a man wants a woman.

C. S. Lewis has some provocative thoughts about this: "Strictly speaking, a woman is just what he does not want. He wants a pleasure for which a woman happens to be a necessary piece of apparatus. How much he cares about the woman as such may be gauged by his attitude to her five minutes after frui-

---

[7] "Sex as Athletics in the Singles Complex," by Roulx, *Saturday Review,* May, 1973.
[8] 1 Cor. 6:13, Phillips.
[9] 1 Cor. 6:18-20.

tion. (One does not keep the carton after one has smoked the cigarettes)."

There's no way for a man to treat a girl as an empty cigarette carton and not devaluate himself and all mankind. Once we regard a person as merely a means to give us pleasure, we are embracing a highly explosive philosophy, one which leads to seeing people as objects. The ultimate conclusion for such a world view is the concentration camp.

As a Christian man yours is a responsible position. You are cast by the Lord in the role of protector of women.

If you're not protecting women today, what right will you have to even hope for protection for your own wife and daughters? A young father I know found he'd been rather amused by such things as the swingles complexes until he thought of his own daughter growing up to live in one. Suddenly it was a whole new ball park!

There are not "good women, bad women, and *your* woman." Not for you, there aren't. God has elevated woman to a much higher position than any feminist ever aimed for, and you have the tough job of helping maintain that position.

Girls often take the initiative in sexual advances.

And this is exactly where your protective role comes in. Can you excuse yourself to your Heavenly Father on the grounds Adam used: "The woman gave me and I did eat"? God didn't let Adam off the hook, and He will not let you off either. It was Eve who was deceived; Adam *knew* it was wrong. The Eves of today are still deceived, thinking they know what the score is.

The roles are mixed and the lines blurred. You will **101**

find it all too easy to get mixed up too, but if *you* take the lead in the temperature of that car, if *you* are the one to say "no" at the end of the evening when she asks you in for a "cup of coffee" (having told you earlier that both parents were away for the weekend), you may give the little lady a huge surprise *and* go up in her esteem about 100 percent. You can be the control figure even in deciding about necking or heavy petting.

One girl wrote me: "It does take two to play Let's See How Far We Can Go Without Going Over the Edge, but only one to stop it. I know it's supposed to be harder for a man to stop, but I've known guys to do it and to go up tremendously in appeal (not just sex appeal) and in my respect. Saying 'no' also confronts a girl with her own self-respect, or lack of it." That's not Grandma Andrews; that's one of your contemporaries and a charming one at that.

All girls are someone special in God's sight even if not in your own.

In the complex interweaving of human togetherness, the God-inspired ideal is surely more than physical oneness. It's a union of interest, of concerned regard for the personhood of the other. Learning to relate to a woman as a person rather than as an object takes some careful rethinking, some prayerful shedding of the snakeskin of media-molded attitudes, and some searching to discover God's ideas on the subject. One of your God-given prerogatives is to help today's mixed-up female to realize her personhood, and surely there should never be a difference in the way you treat a Christian girl and a non-Christian. Christ died for *all*, and you are His representatives here. Some men, having attempted to seduce a girl, then switch to "witnessing" to ease their conscience. It's a lost cause; **102** they have demonstrated what they think of her value.

There's the constant problem of lustful thinking.

This is a universal problem. One thing you *don't* do is say, "No, No. I will not think about this. I will shove it out of my mind. I will not. I will not. I will...."

That focuses your attention on the subject like a Kamikaze pilot zeroing in on a flight deck. I once tried this technique when I was in my teens, and I *still* remember that thought! The old vacuum principle: Concentrate on pushing them out and they rush in "seven times worse." We need to *engage* our minds with something positive. At once. "If you believe in goodness and if you value the approval of God, *fix your minds* on whatever is true and honourable and just and pure and lovely and praiseworthy."[10] *Your* move. You can *choose*. Therein lies your significance.

Verbalized prayer is a strong way of replacing negative thoughts. "Tell God every detail of your needs in earnest and thankful prayer, and the peace of God . . . *will* keep constant guard over your hearts and minds."[11] That's a promise from God. Only if we call God a liar dare we say, "Well, it may work for others, but it won't work for me." God doesn't have favorites; this promise is to *you.*

How's a man to handle a relationship in which the physical has already gotten out of hand? How do we get it back on the right level?

From the beginning, God's standard has been only one man and one woman on a till-death-do-us-part basis. Man *is* fallen, and unfortunately that ideal has long since been obliterated in too many lives. More

---

[10] Phil. 4:8, Phillips.
[11] Phil. 4:6, Phillips.

often than not Christian men and women have had several-to-many sexual experiences ranging from casual encounters to involvements that have left deep scars. We have come so far from God's norms that dealing with the results of today's sexual ethics is like trying to unravel a matted mass of roots in an ancient bog.

To take the stance that physical union alone constitutes marriage seems to me not only unrealistic but non-scriptural. Paul, even as he underlined the seriousness of sexual sin and told the Corinthian men that they became one with a prostitute, did not tell them to marry the woman with whom they had fornicated.

Individual cases are going to vary, naturally. Once having shared sex (even to the extent of heavy petting), it's nearly impossible to return to a platonic level. The more involved you've become, the harder it is. Most couples who are serious about obeying God will find they have to separate and reconsider things prayerfully. Continuing to sleep together while you decide God's leading would be an action hard to defend and would only further befuddle you. God will give strength to do what He asks — always.

If you've been sleeping with a girl, there are some things that need to be weighed carefully. In acting irresponsibly before God, you have acquired certain responsibilities for another human being. These cannot be glossed over. The nature of the association itself comes under consideration: is it a once or twice thing where you've been carried away or is it a long term one with real emotional ties? What about intent? Did you look on this as a permanent alliance when it began? If the girl is a Christian, you need to think hard about what constitutes marriage in God's eyes.

If she is not a Christian and your liaison began when you weren't either, you cannot just shrug it off: "Nice to have known you, but now I'm a Christian, so 'bye.' "

104 On the other hand, there is the seriousness of marry-

ing a non-Christian, which is serious indeed. My own thinking is that a partnership for life with a non-Christian is even more serious than breaking up an existing liaison.

If you began an involvement with a non-Christian after you became a Christian, you are in still deeper water, aren't you? You'll need to be open with the girl, honestly accepting your own share of guilt. The whole question of this girl's attitude to God may be caught in the wheels of your choices.

In all these instances you'll need to back up to the place where you personally went off the rails in your dependence on God. (Never mind her part: God wants to deal with you about your part.) Your choices have brought some painful consequences. Not just to you, but to an irreplaceable human being whom God values.

And you know that God's love and forgiveness cover this, too. His understanding *is* unlimited. Read David's outpouring in Psalm 51. He had done more than sleep with the wrong woman. Murder and treachery were added, yet he called on God with confidence for a new, clean heart.

It seems almost impossible to think God expects us single men never to have intercourse before marriage.

Difficult, certainly. Impossible, no. God doesn't ask the impossible. Remember, if the Christian faith doesn't work here, it doesn't work. And it takes a bigger man to practice abstinence than non-abstinence.

Then is masturbation the only answer till marriage?

This is always a tricky question because Scripture nowhere comes out and makes a plain statement about masturbation. Some feel it is a cobwebbed specter in **105** the shadows that no one should ever mention, let alone practice. At the other pole are those who feel it to be God's safety valve. Without taking a stand that the Scriptures do not seem to take explicitly, let's be realistic:

— There's the power of the mind. If fantasizing can produce orgasm, you have some idea of the power of thought-life. What kind of fantasies would be the stimuli? Would they involve a particular girl, and if so, can this be divorced from lusting after her? Scripture is explicit about lusting being equivalent to the act itself. Fantasies can get so far-out that true sexual experience could be a letdown. One Christian I know found that after his elaborate sex fantasies, his first intercourse meant absolutely nothing. He also found that fantasizing and masturbation led him on to promiscuity which began to affect his work so adversely that it became devoid of meaning.

— Masturbation can be a dark closet of the mind to which the shy and socially inept can withdraw. It's all too easy in your head: no other person's reactions or expectations, no responsibilities.

— For some there could be a different reaction: Rather than easing the tension and *helping* resist temptation, masturbation could make giving in just that much easier when confronted with a flesh-and-blood woman.

— Fantasizing equals emotional involvement which can equal either emotional disturbance or destructive action of some kind. External actions are rooted in the thought-life.

On the other side: If any of you are grinding your own face in the dirt with guilt over this practice, quit being so hard on yourself. While I don't think encouraging people in this practice is sound, the Lord will forgive you and cleanse and help you to overcome **106** in this trouble spot, as in all others. He doesn't stand off in a corner saying, "Well, Jerry, John, Fred, Ian ... get *that* straight and then come back and I'll see about forgiving you." He knows the *only* way we can defeat any problem is to bring it *to Him* to deal with.

You see, your body is valuable to God. He lives there. That fact should make a difference to each one of us in the way we treat our own bodies and the bodies of others.

Most of you are looking forward to having a wife, and perhaps children. Thinking in terms of bringing *them* something of value may act as a deterrent in this whole area of sexual control. What you do now, what you *are* now is going to have a bearing on this. What about when your son says, "But, dad, how did *you* handle this?"

Most of us haven't had that kind of closeness to our dads. I never opened my mouth to mine about sex.

More's the pity. Wouldn't you *like* to have such open communication with *your* son that he'd be free to talk about these things with you?

You're right, I would.

Today's Christian man is in a keen tension between following the majority or being labeled gay. It's an uncomfortable position.

You don't know HOW uncomfortable.

Sex has become the last bastion of the insecure male, the one remaining role in which he feels he can "prove" his manhood.

The sex drive, however, is something you *can* control, with your choice reinforced by God's strength. 107

Either that or you're going to have to plead being a force-driven machine with no power to direct your own life.

God does not expect you to just grit your teeth or join some monastic order and head for the Himalayas. This vital force, properly controlled, can produce an immense output of productive work, perhaps even a masterpiece in your field. It's been done before. Interestingly enough, history seems to demonstrate that when moral depravity and permissiveness take over a culture, the artistic creativity declines in ratio.

Admittedly, you have a real battle in this arena of sexual ethics. In no other quarter are you more battered by a strong consensus pulling you down from God's view of what man is. You will need to sift and analyze all the signals being sent your subconscious from every avenue. You are like a besieged city, surrounded by strategically placed weapons. It will require a serious think-through of what the God-given ethic really is, testing every attitude and viewpoint that comes up against it and making up your own mind about what practical approach you must make to it.

Freedom means choice, and choice is not repression. When you choose God's route for your life, you are enjoying the greatest dignity He confers on the human beings He has created.

Are you driving or driven?

10

The Name Is the Same

Marriage is an institution many now consider as passé as the horse and carriage. *Mademoiselle,* a popular American magazine, sent out a national questionnaire asking women how they felt about marriage. Even to the alert young men who conducted the queries, the answer was "the blockbuster, the eye-opener and mind-blower." Four years ago most women queried were planning on marriage eventually; today's women are overwhelmingly voting against it. Renewable contracts appeal, but marriage is looked upon as one of civilization's great failures.

Many of your contemporaries who may believe in it see it as something apart from and subsequent to a series of sexual frolics of greater or less duration. Grandpa sowed his wild oats, then settled down. If grandma had tried it, she would have been branded for life as a "fallen woman." Today her "liberated" granddaughter competes for prizes in oat-sowing. Marriage, if it comes at all, will come later. Much later. (Just why it should come at all is a question that snags one's attention and points up the contradictions many feel in the "free-life." The reason given by some free-swinging singles is that it's best for children to be brought up in a "real home": i.e., with married partners as parents. Why should this be so if the liberated life is superior?)

In a recent issue, London's *New Society* points out that societies of human beings have always considered sex too explosive to practice without legal restraints and have therefore devised carefully structured social, cultural, and economic regulations which will guarantee the continuity of an ethnic population.

It's easy to see why some *men* might want to duck the altar promenade. From their point of view, when they marry they assume a heavy financial responsibility and possible progeny for which they have little taste. Sex is certainly not the problem: The philosophy of the promiscuous Portnoy boys is, "Why buy a cow when milk is cheap?" Marriage is no longer a requirement for social acceptance (for either men or women), permanency is a "drag," and financially the benefits seem all on the woman's side. (With some places already requiring women to pay alimony when divorced, this is a changing situation.)

Various alternatives are offered: multi-liaisons, "legal" wife-swapping, renewable contracts, and the suburban sport of swinging. Interestingly enough, group marriage is predicted in the Bible where we find seven women pulling at one poor man, offering to maintain themselves financially for the security of his name.[1]

You will need clear-cut convictions about marriage if you are going to be able to stand against the consensus. The current mores are seeping into Christian thinking like color in a tie-dye. We need to know what we *do* believe and why.

---

[1] Isa. 4:1.

What about the view many have that the single life is more spiritual than married life?

This is not the Bible's overall view of marriage. The passage that befuddles many is the one in Corinthians.[2] Some get hung up right away on the first verse: "It is good for a man not to touch a woman."[3] At once we're faced with a question: How does this possibly fit in with other things Scripture states about marriage? But the chapter begins, "Now about those questions you asked in your last letter. . . ."[4] It's apparent Paul is quoting from a letter the Corinthians had written him. These Corinthians, in a reaction against the depraved society out of which they had just come, may have swung to the notion that the more spiritual thing would be not to marry at all. This idea remains prevalent among some sincere contemporary evangelicals, but it presents marriage as a second-rate solution for people who cannot otherwise control their physical drives. That's a poor view of marriage and certainly is a violation of the picture of Christ's relation to the church.

Then in 7:2 Paul does say, "Each man *should* have his own wife,"[5] which would imply something much stronger than permission — an indication of "ought to."

So unless you are absolutely convinced that God has given you the gift of celibacy, don't torment yourself with the idea that to be dedicated you must remain single when everything in you is crying out for marriage. Being able to say "Lord, I am willing to be single if *You* choose" is one thing, but if it *is* His will, He will make it a peaceful thing for you, and you won't go up in smoke.

---

[2] 1 Cor. 7.
[3] 1 Cor. 7:1, KJV.
[4] 1 Cor. 7:1.
[5] 1 Cor. 7:2, RSV.

A lot of us today are wondering what actually constitutes marriage.

Ceremony certainly had little to do with marriage at the start. A man was required to leave father and mother and be joined to his wife "in such a way that the two became one person." This is not a euphemism. If I become a part of one person, I can't add on another person and another and another without becoming a distortion of God's intention.

In the New Testament ethic, Christ elaborates on this and says that what God joins is not to be unlinked by man or man's laws. How archaic such standards are made to sound now! Tragically, we have come a long way from God's ideal.

Why do we bother with a ceremony?

Legal sanction, for one thing. A Christian is supposed to abide by the laws of the land, and while it may not be long before there are no laws governing cohabitation, there are now. In most states in the U.S., for instance, even a common law marriage is not recognized until the partners have been together for quite some time.

The permanency of marriage is designed to protect the home and the personalities of the partners. Human nature being what it is, a change in feelings tempts us to terminate an affair that has no ties. Two people living together may feel bound for life, though most reserve mental loopholes and the couples in free-love arrangements seldom share lifelong togetherness. There is impermanence implied even in thinking, "I *can* pick up and leave if I want to. I have no responsibilities, no financial ties. If I get bored with this chick, I'll go find another." One might argue that it does not matter with 112 "two consenting adults" — *if* God had nothing to say to all this. However, God does not adapt His standards in different times and cultures to the way men *feel* about things.

Marriage also protects children. Society with all its "freedom" can still be cruel to children whose status is not legalized.

All through history, however permissive the sex ethics have been, setting up a new home and family has been a step of real significance, has been a time of joyful celebration. It calls for dancing, fancy clothes, music, flowers — food and drink — whatever the culture equates with joy.

When two Christians marry, they are making a life-time commitment to one another. In addition, their commitment is a demonstration of the indissoluble union of Christ and the Church, of Christ and the be-liever. A Christian ceremony can speak to today's society like a choir of trumpets.

But an ELABORATE wedding ceremony? Why isn't the Justice of the Peace process sufficient?

Legally, it is. This makes me remember the drab county office where I went with my husband-to-be for the required license before our church wedding. The sign on the counter read: "Licenses: Hunting, Fishing, Marriage." In that order.

There is sanctity and wonder in this agreement be-tween human beings. And why not? God is its designer. I'm not saying elaborate ceremonies. Far from it — especially if the couple doesn't have the first month's rent. A simple ceremony can have dignity and charm.

When it comes to weddings, even the most dedicated blue-jeaner can come up with surprises. I remember one shopping in the Swiss city of Lausanne, wearing jeans, a policeman's cape, large hat, and bare feet while munching a whole salami. But for her wedding 113

it was formal white satin. Not all girls are tradition-
alists about their weddings, but most want a unique
day to remember. Traditions often have much common
sense behind them. Taking vows before God and before other Christians (and also before angels and
demons) underlines the responsibility, the lifelongness
of what is being done.

How can a man be sure he's picking the right girl?

Life and fallen human nature being what they are,
he can't. But there are some guidelines that help in
making such an important choice. First of all, the girl
you'd choose would be a Christian. Right?

I know we talked about this before, but I still have questions. If I fall in love with a non-Christian how can she become a Christian if I don't show her real love?

Love has been defined as wanting the best for the
loved one.

Exactly. And the best thing that could happen would be for her to become a Christian, and I'd be trying to help.

Wanting her to know God *is* wanting the best for
her, no question there. The caring would show when
you faced the how-to. I believe the Scripture about
being unequally yoked involves more than marriage;
it touches any deep commitment with a non-Christian.
The closer you tie a girl to you emotionally, the more
you are "yoked" to her. And in the end you could destroy her.

Your girl might be a very honest person. In that case,
114 she would fight Christianity harder than ever because

she would not want to be influenced by *you*. This would make a difficult decision doubly difficult.

Because of your emotional involvement you'd be the last person to help her. The big issue is her becoming a Christian. Could you be unselfish enough to fade out for a while and let someone else help? The girl could then prove *to herself* whether her interest in God and Christ was real. You're only going to complicate matters. Neither of you is made of stone. How much poring over the Bible side by side could you manage and not lose your cool?

But she would need someone to look after her, to guide her.

Of course, but God has many people He can call on.

But if she said she couldn't talk to anyone but me?

Back off a minute and realize how that sounds. Someone experiencing real thirst doesn't say, "I'll only drink from a blue lusterware cup." If it's Truth she's after, she'll go on searching till she finds it, and she will be quite content to talk to another girl, an older woman, or a pastor.

The responsibility would rest on you. God's advice and counsel are available to you in the Scriptures and in prayer; she would have only her own integrity and feelings to go by. No matter how balanced she might seem, you couldn't expect her to have God's viewpoint. None of us can have that without the Holy Spirit. You could not allow yourself to trust her judgment on what would be right in your association. With no disrespect to her as an individual, one has to realize that it's God who says non-Christians are spiritually dead.[6]

---

[6] Eph. 2:1, Phillips.

It's always hard to deal with things as they *are*, not as one wishes them to be. Would you care enough for this girl to demonstrate that Christ is your top priority? Actions *do* speak louder than talk. Could you show her you care enough about her not to confuse or hurt her? This takes courage of a high order, but if she is going to come to the Lord she must decide alone — and she would be much clearer about her commitment without you.

There remains the hard fact that she may *never* become a Christian. The longer your closeness continues, the harder it will be to break up. The pain inherent in such a situation is one consideration in the whole question of dating non-Christians.

Wholeness is, first of all, a matter of one's becoming whole with Jesus Christ. The oneness God intends marriage to be is only possible if a whole man is united with a whole woman. A whole being united to a non-whole being is an abnormality.

Assuming then that the girl I choose is a Christian, what about other priorities?

There is the level of spirituality. Just being a Christian is not all there is to it. If she's a new Christian, one can't predict how she may develop. Suppose you feel God wants you on a mission field. You'll need a partner who will be 100 percent with you. A new Christian might think being a missionary's wife would be romantic, having no idea of what it would involve or of God's calling for her. Or you might find yourself staying at home because of *her* choice and facing a lifetime of guilt. If you are the new Christian and she is very mature spiritually, you have a different set of problems. If you apply yourself to growth and she's careful of your position as leader in the home, such a marriage can be good. But there are potential hazards.

What makes you want to marry a particular girl? Is it only biology? Is it pride in her appearance, her attainments? Is it what she does for *you?* Or is it love? The famous clause about wives submitting to their husbands[7] is followed by "Husbands, show the same kind of love to your wives as Christ showed to the church when he died for her."[8] *Your* command from the Lord is the tougher of the two.

Marriage equals love — and faithfulness — and communication. Two individuals actually become one before God; their relationship should aim toward a practical outworking of that oneness in all departments of life. Marriage is not a self-development course. You are "partners in receiving God's blessings."[9] You will benefit from each other's viewpoints and learn from each other.

Threshing things out is vital — both before marriage and during. If you have trouble communicating *now,* don't expect some magic radar to bring you onto each other's wavelength when married. Even now, you and your girl should be able to discuss everything from birth control to the state of the union.

If the two of you spend most of your free time video-viewing you may need to think about communication. Over the years TV can build up a wall that blocks communication and becomes too thick to shout through.

Discussing *how* to help each other is important in this team effort — each trying to find out what really constitutes helpfulness in the mind of the other. You may zig when she wants you to zag. On the other hand, she may pretty up your workshop with pink ruffled curtains or sort out all "those messy papers" on your desk. Good intentions but jammed signals.

---

[7] Eph. 5:22.
[8] Eph. 5:25.
[9] 1 Pet. 3:7.

Can you laugh together? A sense of humor is of more value than diamonds or gilt-edged stocks.

You'll be sharing much of your precious free time with your wife. Are you "rehearsing" for this phase of married life now or do you regard all your free time as "mine"?

Sometimes a man, seeing himself in the "big protector" role, carries on with a stiff upper lip and shuts his woman out of his problems. Who's kidding whom? Any woman worth her salt knows when something's wrong with her man, and we can stand almost anything better than *not knowing*. We don't really think much of the "Don't worry your pretty little head — let daddy take care of this nasty old problem" gambit. Marriage is sharing.

It may make you feel important to have your girl totally dependent on you, but if you shear her of all her independence you'll have an emotional cripple on your hands.

But I want her to lean on me. I want to do things for her.

Bravo. Except: You will not always be there. You might have trips that take you away. You will have other commitments. She needs some life of her own. She might even outlive you. Women who have become totally dependent on their husbands sometimes collapse when widowed. Give your girl lots of room for growth. To the extent that she's able, let her share your interests, business and otherwise. Her feminine viewpoint can often add new facets to your own.

Your aims in life, your value systems need to be similar. If you're a man who loves the land and animals and she's only happy in the city with lots of people around, it's the yellow caution light.

118   What about interests generally? Are you tuned in to

classical music, lectures, and poetry while she's completely wrapped up in sports? Or the other way round? If she has a deeply absorbing interest such as sculpture or harpsichord playing, that *can* become a threat to a man if it is something he neither shares nor wants to understand. Some difference adds spice, but too much difference spoils the flavor.

What about education?

A Ph.D. *might* marry a girl who didn't make it through grade eight, but it comes close to being a 100-to-1 shot. He'd need to pray a lot.

Don't shrug off background.

Shades of the Victorians!

Too wide a social gap — social, cultural, or racial — can add a great deal to the compexity of marriage. Englishmen, because of their society's class structure, have an even more complicated situation than Americans. The Bible is certainly not against international or interracial marriages, but just be sure if you are considering such a marriage that you're facing all the inherent problems. Love *is* myopic, and waking up one morning to find you have no communication can be scary.

Many of you are thinking seriously of having a truly open home. Keep in mind that the woman has a great deal to do with setting the atmosphere of the home — and not just in decor and flower arrangements. If you treasure the idea of a home where you can bring all kinds of people, a home that is a real showcase for the things you believe, be sure your girl shares this dream. Trying to force a quiet, introspective girl into this slot could cause problems.

What's a good age for marriage?

Marriage is less a question of chronological age than of ability to assume responsibility. Some people are responsible at nineteen, others not even at forty. Current tensions being what they are, younger marriages are worth considering. However, readiness for commitment is important. An astounding number of men, unprepared for the responsibilities, opt out and join the "missing persons" club.

The choice of a wife is second only to the choice of Christ as Savior and Lord. Be careful that when you are ready to marry you don't settle for the first attractive girl who comes along. Marriage is far more than an excuse for legalized sex or an escape hatch from loneliness. Parental pressures (which you men experience as well as the girls) are not good reasons either. Here, as always, the Lord must lead the individual.

While we're on age: We discussed age differences in friendships and dating. What about in marriage?

It needs to be looked at realistically, not romantically. Say you're thirty-eight and the girl is eighteen. I can well understand the attraction, but there will come a day when you are fifty and she's a vibrant thirty. When you're an old man of seventy-five, she'll be fifty-five — not ancient by today's standards. It doesn't take a mathematician to figure out that there will be problems.

Or the other way round? Is it wrong for a man to marry a girl a lot older than he is?

120   Wrong? Certainly not. Dangerous? Yes. (I don't

think I'd want to be the woman worrying about keeping up in looks and every other way with a much younger husband.) A man might have difficulty in maintaining leadership in such a marriage. However, there are exceptional cases that have worked out very well.

What about children? If one of you regards them as "noisy little monsters" and the other cuddles any baby in sight, the whole question of parenthood needs to be considered carefully.

If you want a family, do you think your girl will be a good mother to your children?

That's hardly something I can prove at this point.

No, but you can watch her with other people's children. Not just at a time when she might be showing off, but when she's being herself. Try to catch the vibes when children are around. Notice the children when she's with them. Kids have a God-given radar system.

Then there's sex attraction.

I thought you'd never get to it.

It's vital, but don't go looking through the wrong end of the telescope, will you? Too many of us *start* there. That can blind you. A girl may bowl you over, but her chemistry may be *all* she has for you — a strong physical attraction devoid of meaning. (*Meaning,* I said, not power. It can be about as *powerless* as nitroglycerin.)

There's the other end of our telescope. You have a girl who's "just a friend." Suddenly the relationship can flare into something pretty exciting. Oh, yes it can. Some great teams have begun as "just friends." If *noth-*   121 *ing* happens, *no* lights go on — no need to waste space on *that* contingency.

Some of you would like some good premarital sex talks. Sensible stuff, not pious platitudes. Don't overlook the potential in doctors, pastors, or balanced, loving older couples who have a good marriage going. At least one adviser should be a Christian.

Marriage does not change our fallenness. You will pledge faithfulness, but there's nothing automatic about it. You're living in a pressure cooker society, and the fire under the pot is sex. And there's more than one kind of unfaithfulness: You could stay together for twenty years, never sleeping with anyone else, and be unfaithful in your thought-life, your look-life. Being married is no more a guarantee against temptation than being a Christian is a guarantee against sinning. Conscious choice is still there in both cases. You *choose* the Lordship of Christ moment by moment; you *choose* faithfulness and love and devotion to your wife every day of your life together.

It's possible, you know, to give each other too much freedom. Trust is one thing; placing each other in situations where temptation is just behind the door is stupid. If you frequently ask an attractive man to squire your wife around while you work overtime, or send her to spend the whole summer in the nice cool mountains while you slave in the hot city, you're sending her out into space without a parachute. To neglect your wife in order to buy her more things shows an inverted set of values. (Where *are* our priorities anyhow? Have we so little faith in our God that we feel we can risk one of His best gifts for "monetary security"?) Togetherness is precious, and life is short.

Sex in marriage is to be enjoyed; it's God's gift. The "Song of Songs" verifies this with rich embroidery, and Proverbs says: "Drink from your own well, my son — be faithful and true to your wife. . . . *Let your man-*

122

hood be a blessing; rejoice in the wife of your youth. Let her charms and tender embrace satisfy you. Let her love alone fill you with delight."[10]

However, there can be lust even in marriage.

What? Are you one of those hyper-spirituals who think sex is only for procreation?

Definitely not. But some men, some Christian men, regard their wives as playthings to be had whenever and however they want. Her preferences are unimportant. They may like certain sex practices that are eminently distasteful to their wives, holding that nothing can be wrong between married partners. So long as both are happy, I wouldn't argue that point, but *unless* there is agreement, the man who insists on bizarre practices is treating his wife as a pleasure machine.

Sex in marriage is mutual sharing and consideration. Lust says *Gimme*; love says *I give you.* While Paul does say, "A girl who marries no longer has full right to her own body, for her husband then has his rights to it," he also says, "*In the same way* the husband no longer has full right to his own body, for it belongs also to his wife. So do not refuse these rights *to each other.*"[11] No place for male dominance there.

What if you wind up with a girl who is frigid — who doesn't like sex at all?

When this happens, it's both sad and serious and calls for much gentleness and understanding. It requires time and love and maybe professional help.

One thing bothers me. Do I share my past sex life with my bride-to-be?

---

[10] Prov. 5:15, 18, 19.
[11] 1 Cor. 7:4, 5.

Openness is vital in any close association — nowhere more than in marriage. But before you can be open with your partner about the past, you need to deal with that past before God. You need to begin at the unpopular place of admitting promiscuity as the sin God says it is. If you've been brushing aside the past with light talk about "youthful indiscretions," "trying my wings," "sowing my wild oats," or even "that meaningful relationship," you'll need the courage to ask the Lord what names He gives it. Once having faced this, you must be sure you accept God's forgiveness and forgive yourself as well. We often say, "I can't forgive myself," but what this means is that we don't really believe God has put everything behind Him. If God in His absolute purity and holiness says He has forgiven me, who am I to question this and say I can't forgive myself? This becomes a form of pride: I can't forgive myself because I can't stand it that *I* (of whom I've had such high hopes!) could do such a thing. God says He puts it *all* under the blood of Christ. There is "*no* condemnation awaiting those who belong to Christ Jesus."[12]

Now if you've faced your past and accepted God's unconditional forgiveness and you want to tell your girl about your past, you will at least be sure your motive isn't that of unloading your guilt feelings on her to ease your own conscience. (And sharing your past shouldn't include names and gory details, by the way.) It's hard to generalize in the realm of human relationships, especially in the intimate and permanent one we call marriage. No one can design a blueprint for you, and there may be situations where not sharing is wise. But it's important for you to be known as the person you *are*. Without masks. You'll have a deeper and freer relationship if you dare to share with one

---

12 Rom. 8:1.

another who you really are. It may seem a perilous experiment —

What if she rejects me?

— but there are two things worth considering: 1) If she's going to reject you on these grounds, how much more tragic the results will be if it all comes out after several years of marriage and she *then* rejects you. 2) When the significant others of our lives know us *as we are* and love us anyway — we are free! This kind of accepting love brings healing and confidence.

Are you prepared to give as well as receive here? Are you ready to be as accepting and understanding with your fiancée as you'd like her to be with you?

I guess every man hopes his bride will be a virgin.

Maybe you need to ask yourself if you are being either realistic or fair. We both know that, unfortunately, few girls today reach twenty with their virginity intact. The girl you'll want to marry will have grown up in the same ugly, permissive society that you have, with virtually all the same "freedoms" and tensions. Do you have the right to demand that the girl you marry be a virgin, especially if you yourself have been promiscuous? There's no double standard in Christ's teachings. You may be the one God uses to assure her of His forgiveness and acceptance.

Marriage is not an *event* in a man's life; it will shape that life. Be sure you don't visualize your wife as an adjunct to your life and career — one more thing you own.

I wish I could write this next in red letters: *Do give each other time!* Don't rush into marriage as if you were going on a vacation. Get to know each other. Since marriage is for keeps, you can afford to deliber- **125** ate; a lifetime's quite a while. Don't be deluded into thinking that today's mores make the situation any more open-ended than it ever was. "No man must ... separate what God has joined together"[13] was stated by your Lord, not by your pastor, your denomination, or me. When Christians take marriage vows, they take them before God. He hears and will make it possible to carry them out. Once married, it is up to you two to prayerfully *make* it last. It will have its ups and downs, its disappointments and disillusionments, but marriage is a living organism, and with care it should become more beautiful as the years go by.

Looking realistically at the subject, C. S. Lewis once said that we do not vow to go on feeling so madly excited about each other for a lifetime (Who could stand it?), but we do vow to remain faithful and to love — a different thing.

I'm shaken by the number of Christian marriages I see coming apart at the seams.

So am I. As I've thought about this, some of the reasons for it that come to mind are:

— the lack of criteria coupled with carelessness. If you men go out to buy a car, you have a clear idea of what you want and what you do not want. You do not grab the first car you like. I'm not equating girls with machines, but if you marry the first girl who sends your blood pressure up or the girl who makes *you* feel great when you walk around with her draped over your arm, you are treating her with less consideration than a car.

— lack of communication. This ranks high on the list. Establishing real communication before marriage, sharing your points of view and your differences is

[13] Matt. 19:6, Phillips.

very important, as we've discussed. If you cannot do it before, you probably won't afterwards. And you can't make love *all* the time.

— a conscious or subconscious reservation that "if this doesn't work, I can always get out of it." The false standards of today's thinking nibble at the Christian ethic through all media. Young couples are often unaware of the attrition until their foundations cave in.

— failure to resolve hang-ups with parents. The child-parent relationship goes so deeply into our psyche that if there are major difficulties here they carry over into almost every other phase of life. Leaping into marriage is no resolution of parental hangups. To the extent that the resolution depends on you, on your own attitudes and honesty, on your love, on your forgiveness, on shouldering the responsibility for your own failures, resolve those hangups.

Your insurance in marriage will be maintaining your vertical relationship with the Lord Himself. Only He can fill in *all* the empty spaces; only *He* understands you totally all the time. But don't you see — this takes the pressure off both you and the girl. If Christ has priority, then neither of you will put the other on a pedestal; you will not bring on that human partnership a pressure it was never intended to bear. Don't try to be a perfect husband. *Expect* some failures and disappointments, and when they come you won't need to say, "Wrong girl"; you will know it's part of her finiteness and your own.

No one can tell you who is right for you but the Lord Himself. He not only can but will, *if you want to hear*. In a field as unpredictable as a life partnership, we dare not go without the Lord's wisdom and direction. He not only knows who you are today (and who she is), but who you both will be ten years from now. You are complete in Him.

But only in Him.

11

Forever Gay?*

Let me start this chapter by saying that I do not write from some pedestal, marble or plastic. Scripture says we are *all* fallen. There is rottenness in our bones from the day we are born, and our particular *symptoms* of that rottenness depend on background, heredity, training, environment, and a multiplicity of other things. I believe that in every one of us there is the potential for just about anything. We cannot know our total capacity for sin. Given the "right" (i.e., the

---

* I write this chapter "on my knees" because I am aware of the seriousness of the problem and of my own limitations. In dealing with homosexuality I know I am dealing with an ultra-sensitive area that we Christians have sometimes avoided, sometimes oversimplified — one so shrouded in the trappings of contemporary thinking that it is difficult to approach with anything like a fresh view.

I want to write directly to the man who considers himself a homosexual; therefore, the conversations will be with him.

For the sake of convenience and writing flow I will sometimes refer to "the homosexual" or "the gay man" although I have serious doubts (discussed further on) that these are valid "tags" for the man whose problem is homosexuality.

wrong) pressures, temptations, deprivations, we do not know what we would do. Personally I have had to come to the flattening awareness that *my* heart is the one Jeremiah is talking about when he says, "The heart is the most deceitful thing there is, and desperately wicked."[1] Any victories in my life have been God's, and, being a slow learner, I've had many failures.

If we Christians think homosexuality does not concern us, that it's a dusky area that could never touch *our* lives, we are being either naive or cruel. Naive because this *is* a problem that involves many Christians, and cruel because by ignoring the homosexual or condemning him out of hand we are neither showing the compassion of Christ nor are we being in the least helpful.

Well, I'm ready to listen, but what are you going to say about us that everybody hasn't said already? I've heard Christians talk about all this. They either align themselves with the trend that says we're all sick, or they condemn us as beyond the pale and draw up their togas as we pass.

Let's look at what society in general is saying. What's happened, of course, is that homosexuality has come out of the men's washrooms, gone through the chic city bedrooms, and is now almost stage center — spotlights, camera! As long ago as 1967 the Episcopal church decided that the homosexual act is "morally neutral" and that a "homosexual relationship between two consenting adults should be judged by the same criteria as a heterosexual marriage; that is, whether it is intended to foster a permanent relationship of love." (Thus Canon Talter Denis of the Cathedral of St. John the Divine, New York City, as reported in the *Denver Post*.) In 1963 an English Quakers' committee reported

---

[1] Jer. 17:9.

that "homosexuality is a natural, morally neutral condition, no more to be deplored than left-handedness in respect to right-handedness."

There are large gay churches that solemnize "holy unions." There are gay bars. Homosexuality is in, and its promulgators, among them many talented artists, musicians, and writers, have led infatuated followers into the boxwood maze because they're *who* they are or because they have done it with flair.

But listen to one of the most gifted leaders in this category: After nearly being killed by one of his frustrated satellites, Andy Warhol, whose dark star drew the "in" crowd of the sixties, recently said: "Since I was shot everything is such a dream to me. I don't know what anything is about. . . . I wasn't afraid before. And having been dead once, I shouldn't feel fear. But I am afraid. I don't understand why."

Can this be Andy Warhol, the master of passive power, the young genius of decadence who ruled a kingdom of other gay boys in the ersatz silver of The Factory? Of course it glittered; the path to darkness is forever studded with synthetic stars.

By contrast, there are thousands caught in this way of life who live it with anything but flair, who daily and hourly suffer deep pangs of guilt, feeling trapped and hopeless — who because of their temperament or background would rather die than be found out. It is in this latter group that we usually find the Christian gay man.

Besides endorsing homosexuality, society says:

1. that the condition is not the person's fault
2. that except in rare cases, it is an *irreversible* condition
3. that it is a condition which cannot be controlled by the individual (i.e., that it must, in some way, be actualized)

4. and sometimes it says that homosexuality is as normal as heterosexuality.

So today's homosexual finds the ground sliced right out from under him at the outset.

Like so many of the rest of us, he is silenced by some psychoanalysts who represent the Delphic oracle for our generation. Some of these experts have decided that it's all an illness. People are "made that way," or they become that way involuntarily. "And that's the diagnosis, Mr. Jones. As for the prognosis, the best we can do is help you to become a better-adjusted homosexual. After several years of one-hour sessions, five days a week, we may bring you to an understanding of *why* you are this way. Twelve thousand dollars, please."

So what else is new? Isn't this just what society is saying about almost all our problems? Apply those four statements above to nymphomania, sadism, child-rape, bisexuality, or kleptomania — today's thinking puts it all into the same pot at the back of the stove, stirs it with impressive psychological degrees, and serves up a witch's brew of confusion, despair, and negativism.

To divest a man of responsibility for his choices is to downgrade him into insignificance. The scriptural view of man is that he is of *vast* significance — every man on earth. He is made in God's image.

We homosexuals?

The image of God is distorted in you *as it is in all of us.* Before the Fall, Adam was a limited but *un*-distorted image of God, but now we are all terrifyingly twisted and marred. So, though scarred by the Fall 131 with the rest of us, certainly the homosexual has been created in God's image. Some of us, because of greater environmental advantages, better heredity, or absence of trauma in childhood, seem less marred or less noticeably twisted, but two things obtain for all mankind if the Scriptures are to be understood literally:

1. *All* men are created in God's image.
2. *All* men are fallen.

Therefore, *all* men need redemption.

What are the origins of homosexuality? Many different reasons are given for a man's choosing sexual experiences — implicit or explicit, real or fantasized — with his own sex. Generally speaking, it takes a strong force to divert a person's normal sexual direction.

Some possible reasons:

— strong fears of heterosexual relationships.

— an all-male background or environment where the child is reared by men, virtually separated from women (in some cases if the environment becomes more normal, the man's sexual orientation could tend to become normal).

— continued failures or disappointments in male-female relationships.

— inordinate attachment to the mother, leading to identification with her.

— a mother who is overly intimate, domineering, possessive, and emasculating with a father who is weak, perhaps detached, unloving, even hostile. (Here, the mother is not assuming *her* God-given role in relationship to the father. Once the scriptural norms are ignored, the tendency in succeeding generations is downward. This holds true in any category.)

— son substituting as "wife" in a motherless home.

— being exposed to sanctimonious attitudes towards sexual things, when mother is severe and sexually unresponsive to father but seductive with son and possibly
132 resentful of his heterosexual relationships.

— sex information given evasively or in a constrained and formal way, combined with distortion in the sexual relationship and roles of father and mother.

— a hunger for *experience*. ("After all, what else *is* there?") This can occur when a man's sexual appetite becomes jaded by heterosexual overindulgence.

— general rebelliousness expressing itself in rejection of societal norms, which would include those relating to sexuality.

Wow! Those reasons hit a lot of guys.

The impact of these causes would vary. Obviously not every man with one of the backgrounds mentioned is going to become a homosexual.

Notice that none of these allow for a person's just "being born that way." (There are the very few hermaphrodites, but this brings up a subject which must be related to rather differently. I would like to speak just to the much wider problem of homosexuality.)

Whatever may have been the childhood influences predisposing a man to homosexuality, it is usually understood that these influences are later greatly reinforced by many conscious choices. Today's ties are rooted in personal pleasure and emotional bonds that have been acquired through choices.

Becoming gay is often the outcome of a despairing search for love in a life style that usually substitutes physical attraction and infatuation for genuine caring. Greco and Wright, studying ten homosexual boys in a correctional institution, found "that at some time in their early life all ten of the affected boys had been in serious need of emotional and social support. An attachment was formed at this time to a man who gave security, understanding, and comfort. When this friend seduced the child it was accepted because of the deep affection for the man and the fear of losing his pro- **133** tection. To each child this relationship was at first distasteful and was recognized as immoral. In some, continuation of the perversion led to pleasure and satisfaction; in others it continued only as a means of obtaining emotional security. In each instance, the homosexual relationship became important after the loss of the cherished friend."[2]

In such a blind-alley search the person can be destroyed. Love involves freedom and *respect* for the loved one and for oneself.

Although there are gay boys who appear outwardly comfortable, especially if surrounded by an approving sub-culture, many homosexuals, whether active or passive, sporadic or confirmed, suffer intensely.

"However strongly they protest their freedom from conventional morality, sex deviants cannot escape a lurking guilt. The fact that many decent folk regard them as moral lepers renders them furtive and unsure or else forces them into flaunting bravado. Though they wear no visible crutches, their disability is real enough."[3]

No wonder the old saw, with its black humor, goes, "Show me a happy homosexual, and I'll show you a gay corpse."

Society at large is busy telling the homosexual, and the gay boys are telling each other, that there is no guilt attached. "I am gay and I make that affirmation with joy and pride. I am a good person," is a remark appearing in *Trends* and quoted in *Christianity Today* (28 September 1973). In the same article Rev. James E. Sandmire, pastor of the Metropolitan Community Church of San Francisco, says, "I'm a gay man and a

---

[2] Harry Bakwin and Ruth M. Bakwin, *Behavior Disorders in Children,* 4th ed. (Philadelphia: W. B. Saunders Company, 1972), p. 496.

[3] Donald J. West, *Homosexuality* (London: Duckworth & Co., Ltd., 1955), p. 153.

minister." He goes on to say that he would be going home that night to his lover of many years and would be preaching the next day and administering communion, "and I think God and I will feel quite good about it."

The church today is talking of love but is failing in just that — in tough love. In the long run, acceptance overlaying unresolved guilt harms the individual. It was Christ who said, "If you love me, obey me."[4]

Over and over in quotes from self-justifying gay men, one is struck with the emphasis on *feeling*. It is the catchword of our time. Nothing is said about thinking or about measuring rods in the moral realm or, in the case of gay ministers, in the spiritual realm.

In the Far East, long removed from Christian influence, homosexuality is an accepted, even amusing way of life. The West, whose culture has been based on Christianity, until recently has considered homosexuality deviant behavior. At one time it was illegal in both the U.S. and England. English common law, the basis for both our legal systems, was founded on the Christian ethic, which in turn was based on Jewish laws. Today, with this foundation badly eroded, in both countries homosexuality is becoming legal between "consenting adults." God's laws, based on His changeless character, set the limits within which man can be fulfilled. One cannot speak of loving God and hating His commandments. God created woman for man, not man for man.[5] It is He who says homosexuality is wrong.

He really does?

In both Old and New Testaments. "Thou shalt not

---

[4] John 14:15.
[5] 1 Cor. 11:9; Gen. 2:18.

lie with mankind as with womankind: it is abomination. . . . If a man also lie with mankind, as he lieth with a woman, both of them have committed an abomination: they shall surely be put to death; their blood shall be upon them."[6] In Romans 1, homosexual attachments are called "vile affections." We'll look at that passage in more detail later.

In addition to frustration and guilt there are inherent dangers for the homosexual, although these have not often been real deterrents. There is the venereal disease problem. Also, because of his vulnerability, the gay man becomes an easy target for blackmail. Exposure has meant the end of some bright careers. Hitler's blood purge of homosexuals in Nazi Germany represents the ultimate in discrimination.

Doesn't one need medical qualifications to deal with homosexuality?

It seems to me that we Christians have bowed too long and too reverently in the technological temples of the professional psychologist or psychiatrist. Some of these people are themselves in the process of revamping pet theories and turning some of their sacred cows out to pasture! As Christian laymen and women we sometimes have had an unholy fear of trampling on "their" ground. At times, rather than speaking loud and clear because of what God's Word says, we've retreated with "No, I'd better leave that to the professional."

Now I am *not* saying that *all* Christians, just because they are Christians, are equally competent to deal with all problems in this world. (Certainly if a Christian counselor finds himself with a deep aversion to the gay boy, he'd better not talk with him.) Nor am

[6] Lev. 18:22; 20:13, KJV.

I saying that *any* nonprofessional is as good for some things as a Christian professional *if he presents his opinions and his Christian beliefs as a unified whole.* Sadly, the number of "reborn" psychiatrists is few. What is more disheartening is that *of* those few, there seems to be a discouraging number who separate their professional procedures from their Christian faith as if the two were in no way connected.

If career and faith are not fused into an integrated unit, there's a short-circuit somewhere. Whether we are ditchdiggers, artists, doctors, philosophers, ballplayers, or university professors, our world view, rock-founded on Scripture, should permeate both work and life style. Without discounting the valuable work done by some psychologists and psychiatrists, perhaps we need to rethink our attitudes toward the great specialist-worship of our age.

Don't some men achieve lasting emotional satisfaction in a homosexual relationship?

Permanent relationships do occur, but they seem to be much in the minority and often explode. One of my Christian friends lived with a man for several years, and their gay friends were amazed that they "made it." (They later broke up.) A brilliant man wrote me, "I had some close relationships — they are gone like the summer." If any of you are familiar with the published diaries of the gay American composer Ned Rorem,[7] you have sensed the terrible pain underlying the breakup of meaningful relationships. Without legal or economic ties, without children, often without social sanction, these relationships are under great stress.

Homosexuality is not new. The Greeks admired it;

---

[7] Ned Rorem, *Paris and New York Diaries of Ned Rorem* (New York: Avon Books, 1970).

the Romans were undermined by it. The men of Sodom have given their name to abnormal sex, and they lived some 1000 years before Christ.

That the Christian answer would be in a different category from any other is based on the fact that our answer revolves totally around the Christian presuppositions: that God exists, that He is personal and loving (therefore interested) and infinite (therefore able), that in the Scriptures He has clearly expressed His thoughts, and that His Son died and rose. This is not the place to defend Christianity. Most of you reading this already believe it. However, without this foundation, the Christian counselor has no more to offer than the deterministic advisers or the relativistic anything-you-think-is-O.K.-for-you-is-O.K. philosophers — and that's not much.

The Bible says that the practice of homosexuality is sinful and against nature — the man's nature. This is good news for the homosexual.

GOOD news?

Yes, because if you tell a man he is incurably "ill," predetermined to live in any private hell in which he finds himself, you predestine him to remain chained. But tell the man he is sinning against God, and you give him hope.

Sounds like "doublethink" to me.

At first confrontation it may seem more discouraging than hopeful. Sin? What an unpopular word! How quaint! How old-fashioned! But since God is and has an unimpeachable moral character which He has revealed to us, then we have a straight edge against **138** which to measure ourselves. If the divine Son did *not* come, if His life was *not* extinguished, if He did *not* rise again, then as Paul saw in the first century, "We *are* of all men most miserable." There is no hope, life *is* absurd, and the faster we slide down the chute into blackness the more exciting the ride.

"But now *is* Christ risen!" Paul's shout, ringing against the rough stone of Nero's prison, resounds into our century, our town, our need today. *"Sin shall not have dominion over you!"* Christ's victory becomes yours.

God's valuation of the individual is most dramatically shown him at the cross. Christ died for sinners — yes, but Christ died for *you*. If homosexuality is a sin — and it is — then this, too, has been dealt with at Calvary. "For God took the sinless Christ and poured into him our sins. Then, in exchange, he poured God's goodness into us."[8]

Mind-blowing? It is. Who but God could engineer that kind of metamorphosis?

You who are struggling with homosexuality have a great thing going for you: your essential maleness.

My what?

The Bible says that in the beginning God created man — male *and* female. *Together* they formed Man, but each half was essentially different from the other half. Even now, after the Fall, there remains this essential maleness or femaleness in the human body from birth.

You who consider yourselves homosexuals are marred by sin as we each are, but *essentially* you have been created male. ("Absolute" sex is chromosomally determined at the moment of conception.) Romans 1:25 says that man changed "the truth of God into a

---

[8] 2 Cor. 5:21.

lie." Part of the "truth of God" in this particular application could be this essential maleness and femaleness. The farther away from this we get, the more we find ourselves in trouble.

In Romans, Paul speaks of men who "deliberately forfeited the truth of God and accepted a lie. . . . God therefore handed them over to disgraceful passions. Their women exchanged the normal practices of sexual intercourse for something which is abnormal and unnatural. Similarly the men, turning from normal intercourse with women, were swept into lustful passions for one another. . . . receiving, of course, in their own personalities the consequences of sexual perversity."[9]

In the Romans passage the word translated normal or natural is the Greek word *physis,* meaning that which is given. It is seldom used in the New Testament, and in this passage it is used only in the discussion of perversion: a distortion of the natural order, of the given. That which is given goes beyond the appearance of a thing to the very core of its nature as God created it.

But I AM gay!

Start with the presupposition that God created you to be a man, not a hybrid. Behind all the twistings, strains, and tensions that have brought you where you are today, the fact remains: God made you a man, a man of great significance who's going to live forever.

God never asks us to do the impossible. Hard things, yes. But He never asks us to do something He is not going to give us power, *His* power, to do. Since He says the practice of homosexuality is sin, then He is not going to leave you out on a limb. He is going to help you obey Him.

---

140   [9] Rom. 1:25-27, Phillips.

As a man released by Christ, you need not be ruled by an obsession with sex. With Christ's life *in you*, working through *the whole man,* you need not walk alone ever again. Since Scripture promises deliverance and victory over sin, then this must apply to you whose problem is homosexuality. Otherwise, this must be the *only* sin from which there is no deliverance, an aspect of fallenness fenced off by itself.

My objection to the usual Christian approach to this subject is that it is treated as if it were at the very top (or bottom) of some categorical chart of sins, and that while the alcoholic, the womanizer, the tax-cheat, the wife-beater, and the proud pharisee are all free to expect deliverance from their particular hangups, we say to you: "You, my friend, must learn to live as a cripple. You are a second-class citizen. It's a fallen world, and we do know you have a rough time ahead, but that's your cross." In what way, then, do we differ from the psychoanalyst who, after years of expensive therapy, sends the homosexual out to be a "better-adjusted homosexual"?

The alternative?

I realize it's dangerous to oversimplify in dealing with *any* particular sin. The personality, the background, the quality and intensity of the scarring and fallenness, the *willingness* to change — all of these things have to be taken into account. Time is surely a factor. But in *all* sinfulness, not just homosexuality. With your God-given maleness, abetted by God's determination for your wholeness, I think it's unfair to withhold from you gay men the message that there is hope for you, too — always, always, *always* under the power of the blood of Christ, of the resurrected Lord and the Holy Spirit. Paul wrote: "We are no longer slaves, but God's own sons. . . . Christ has made 141 us *free*."[10] Should he have added: "This does not apply to homosexuals. Abandon hope, all ye who are in this class"?

In another part of this book we've discussed avoiding the occasion for sin and not putting oneself in situations that bring undue stress. A heterosexual man has to have the wisdom and the grace of God to stay out of situations that put too great a strain on him. If he does not and falls into trouble, we don't expect him to go around announcing, "I couldn't help it" or "Satan pushed me." For the gay man the same thing applies. Since certain jobs and professions have a high incidence of gay people, the Christian whose weakness is in this area ought to think carefully before taking up, or returning to, such tempting situations. This also means giving up favorite hangouts.

But what ABOUT my sex drive? Does God expect me to practice total abstinence?

Would you say that the heterosexual man, with the flaunting temptations all around, *must* periodically have sex with girls?

It's certainly the consensus.

Yes, but as a Christian, *you* say — ?

As a Christian I have to take the position that since it is forbidden, God will give the guy strength to abstain till marriage. Otherwise, God will give him a successful and fulfilled life without sex.

No matter how long he has to wait?

Right.

[10] Gal. 4:7; 5:1.

Admitting the immense difficulties, do you think God can do this?

The Bible says there's nothing impossible with God — Oh!

Since you're equally as important to God, fully as significant, as much loved as any other individual on God's earth, we have to assume that you are equally responsible. Please don't overlook your own choices. It's an established fact that many practicing homosexuals begin playing in their heads long before they ever do anything overtly. I think we take one more layer of humanity from men when after saying, "You can't help *being* what you are," we follow this by saying, "You have no control over your *actions*." This is to denigrate them into performing seals.

Today's thinking insists that a homosexual must give in to his sex drives. It also says that the heterosexual man must pursue *his* sex drives: an unmarried man is expected to be promiscuous; a married man will probably be adulterous.

As Christians we cannot say this. The heterosexual man in Christ has the privilege of marrying, the freedom to be monogamous; he is not to be a slave to his body's demands. Or he may choose to be unmarried and remain chaste. Is there, then, a chaste homosexual? If chastity means not being involved in a physical relationship, I'm sure that there have been many. But it seems to me we trip over the well-known dilemma horns here. We say on one hand, "O.K., *be* a homosexual as long as you do not practice the perversion explicitly." But throughout the whole of Scripture we are confronted with the power of the thought life: "The thought of foolishness is sin." "As he thinketh . . . 143

so is he." "Anyone who looks . . . with lust . . . has already committed. . . ."[11]

Since this is so, can we say that just *non*-practice of physical acts (normal *or* homosexual) is enough? What about those thoughts, fantasies, desires? What *about* bringing every thought into the captivity of Christ?[12] Isn't the problem similar for both classes of men?

Well, if thinking equals doing, why fight it?

A distinction has been made, correctly, between practicing homosexual acts and non-practice just as we make a distinction between the normal man who lives promiscuously and the normal man who lusts but does not activate his lust. Socially, the difference is considerable. But in the case of the non-practicing homosexual, though we may strenuously deny determinism on every other level, we seem to feel that *he* is more or less predetermined to *be* what he is; he just has to behave himself. The consensus seems to be that as long as our Christian gay man does not engage in actual physical activity, he's not to be censored any more. He is, of course, to be pitied — a sad sort of anti-hero who has made some admirable adjustments but is still, well now, really, a bit — you know — not like *us*. With his low self-image, the homosexual needs such an attitude like a perforation in his cranium.

My mind questions all this. Does Scripture ever discuss homosexuality apart from its practice? In fact, does it ever speak of "a" homosexual as an entity apart from homosexual actions? In Romans 1 there is a progression in action, a downward spiral. Speaking of people in revolt against God, Paul says: "God let them go ahead into every sort of sex sin, and do whatever

---

11 Prov. 24:9; 23:7, KJV; Matt. 5:28.
12 2 Cor. 10:5b, KJV.

they *wanted* to [desire] — yes, vile and sinful things with each other's bodies [actualizing the desire]." Then: "God gave them up unto vile *affections* [the heart] and the men . . . burned with *lust* [inside] for each other . . . *doing* shameful things [outside]. . . ."[13]

Thought, as always, gets into the scene first; action becomes the outgrowth of thought. Once entered into, this can become a vicious circle: thoughts leading to actions, actions leading to despairing thoughts leading to more action, and so on.

Are you saying that even if a man is not going to practice homosexual acts, it's wrong for him to be attracted to his own sex? How can he help it? Recently I read a very moving book by a Christian homosexual. He was crystal clear in his theology but suffered much pain over his attraction to another Christian man.

This is a very sensitive area. God forbid that I should foist on you any cheap ideas, false hopes, or simplistic solutions of my own. But I cannot believe that the God I know and worship will say, "No, you must not *do* this thing," and then leave you starving for the rest of your life, hankering after forbidden fruit. What kind of deliverance is that? Most of the cured alcoholics I've known know better than to take the first drink, but that's not the same as a constant craving for alcohol.

Any Christian who is honest before God knows that he has sinned much more in his mind and heart than he ever has outwardly. We hate to admit it — indeed, many of us *won't* admit it — but if "the thought of foolishness is sin" and looking with lust *is* adultery — well, who can throw stones? I think lots of us need a deep look into our own thought and emotional life to

[13] Rom. 1:24; 1:26, KJV; 1:27.

see that in God's sight (even if not in society's) we are as deeply dyed as anyone.

But so many times a thought hits me before I'm even aware —

There remains, of course, the distinction between temptation and sin. A thought knocking on the door of our mind is not sin; it's when we invite it to come in and sit down and we bring out the refreshments that it's wrong.

In Romans 1:31 (KJV) it speaks of people who were without "natural affection." An absence of natural (given) affection leaves us open to the unnatural. Speaking of the rebellious Israelites, God said: "I gave them up unto their own hearts' lust."[14]

So the HEART can lust as well as the body?

You see, I think this hits us all. Whether we fret over singleness, whether we feel deprived and sorry for ourselves because of a relationship renounced "for God," or whether we desire a member of our own sex — we covet. Scripturally, uncontrolled desire for something God has said "no" to is equated with idolatry.

The normal man's heart can lead him wrongly, even though he breaks no rules of society. For instance, a young Christian (or one not so young) can find himself strongly attracted to someone else's wife. (Oh, yes, he can. Remember David.) Our man may never say a word, may never lay a finger on the lady, he may even leave town, but if he fantasizes a physical relationship, if he gets sensual pleasure in his thought of her, he's in trouble. It was the Lord Himself who said

146   [14] Ps. 81:12, KJV.

that in His sight this equals committing adultery in his heart. God takes our thought-life seriously.

If we give you gay men your due as being equally significant before God and therefore equally responsible, then falling in love with a male friend or playing with ideas in your mind is in the same category.

"Don't let the world around you squeeze you into its own mould, but *let God* [choice again] re-mould your minds *from within*."[15] Do you see where the emphasis lies? Your choice is to seek God's work inside you. Then you *allow* God to do what is needed — the whole re-molding bit. Can *you* alter this pattern made up of an uncountable number of threads, woven into the very tapestry of your inner self? *You cannot. But God.* . . . God can; He wants to; He is able. He has done it in other gay lives. Let me quote from a letter from a healed homosexual I know well.

> This whole area is certainly being placed in a position that will soon make it one of the main sins of this day. I know so clearly that we first must call this, as with similar problems, *sin* and then immediately and simply unfold our Lord Jesus Christ's full provision with His blood covering the redeemed new man. I am so certain that in dealing with this area we have employed human analyses more than that simple place of claiming and experiencing our Father's healing. Sexual sin is not an overwhelming impossible situation in our Father's eyes. It is just another one of the sins He has taken care of and wants to prove Himself through. Also, we must not make any compromises in this area: God does not. If we are washed in the blood of our Lord Jesus Christ then we, as a believer, are calling Him a liar if we are not experiencing that healing in our life. Of course, we grow in our realization of this as we grow in Him each day. I don't mean to imply instant holiness! Yes, the temptations will come and go but they have nothing to do

---

[15] Rom. 12:2, Phillips.

> with the healing we received at the Cross. We are
> commanded to walk forth now in the resurrection
> life of our Lord and Saviour. The thing that bothers
> me most with Christians dealing in this area are the
> numerous milk-toast compromises. God demands *flee-
> ing* and rejoicing in our walk. Amen.

No theorizing here. Of course, there is tension and
temptation at times. Being healed is a continuing
process.

There are others: among the more dramatic are a
male prostitute, free after seven years of up and
down experience with the Lord and a transvestite
who's recovered his manhood.

Some of you have struggled manfully for years, fully
convinced that the best you can hope for is nonpractice
and that you are doomed to constant frustration in this
vital area of your humanity. Others of you, filled with
self-loathing, continue to get caught in participation.

Is this the one sin Christ's death did not have victory
over? *Did* Paul exempt this when he said, "Sin shall not
have dominion over you"? (He lived in the debauched
Roman world; he certainly was conversant with homosexuality as a fact of life.) Are verses about victory,
triumphant Christian living, joy, and the rest for all
Christians but you?

Christ's victory was *for all*. He took on Himself *all*
our negatives and the twistedness of our total personalities. One Christian gay boy wrote to me: "For a long
time I thought that God dealt only with the spiritual
and man had to work the rest out for himself . . .
despair for me!" No. But it's not self-effort. "If you try
to be justified by the Law" — if you try to deliver yourself by your own efforts — "you automatically cut yourself off from the power of Christ, you put yourself outside the range of his grace."[16]

[16] Gal. 5:4, Phillips.

In no sense am I promoting Christian perfection. We *all* stumble and fall, and to a certain extent always will. The married man never knowing a moment's lust for another woman, the single man never tempted, the Christian homosexual never again feeling the pull — no, I am not saying this will occur before the Lord comes back. But God *promises* healing, deliverance, and wholeness — certainly not *less* to the homosexual than to others.

Time is a vital factor. For some men the pattern stems from so far back, the behavior (or thought) patterns are so deeply ingrained and women are so repulsive that *much* time and patience will be required. Quite a lot would depend on the man's relationship with the Lord, his courage, his persistence, the genuineness of his *desire* for healing. But these latter things only open the door. *God* has to do the changing. As in other areas of Christian victory, it's willingness first and then the claiming of Christ's resurrection life.

One of my sadder memories is hearing a gifted young gay Christian say to me, "I know Christ can heal me. I just don't think I want Him to. I *like* my life."

I think for many of you there is far more hope of normal living than you have allowed yourself to imagine. But please consider that healing *does* begin with a *desire* to be healed. Christ said to Bartimaeus, the blind man, in Mark 10:51: "What do you *want* me to do for you?"

God asks us for only one step at a time. Any of you who have ever walked in thick fog know that the only way you can penetrate its density is by moving into it. One step gives you some visibility for the next step. Have the courage to take just one small step; the Lord is ahead in the fog.

Homosexuality is sometimes seen as a defense mechanism needing to be dealt with as other neurotic 149 fears need to be dealt with. A gay man may be retreating from something even more deeply rooted than his fear of heterosexual experience. Such a person needs help in uncovering what *that* fear is. For many of us, our fears and special phobias, repellent and painful as they are, are our familiar emotional canes. They defend us from still worse fears. We say, "This may not be God's best; it may not be of God at all. But it's mine, all mine, and I can't let it go."

Sounds familiar.

In George Orwell's novel *1984* all the prisoners were terrified mindless of the mysterious "Room 101" which turned out to contain the *one* thing that each man dreaded above all else in the world, a fear diabolically discovered by his torturers. Each of us may have his own Room 101. "Can't help it. I'm just that way. I'll always be terrified of the dark, afraid of airplanes, unable to face high places. That's *me*. That's what I have to live with." And we can and do limp through life with fears we dare not entrust to the God of the subconscious. We dread the cure more than the disease. Our own special fear continues to eye us out of dark corners. Many of these phobias are not as vital as the great life-surge of sex, but *God* is the same.

What about it? You who battle with *this* aspect of fallenness, you who feel you must grope through life twisted and torn up inside: Can you, in the deepest place of your heart, your emotional vault, your guts — *dare* you entrust this to your heavenly Father, to the Christ who answered for *this* thing in your life? Dare you say, "Take it. Take the ideas, the longings, the attractions. You deal with them. I believe that Your victory on the cross was for me, too. I believe my identity need not be wrapped up in this package. I **150** know it will take time. I'll have my ups and downs. I'll probably fall flat in thought, if not in practice, but I believe You mean it when You say You want me to be whole."

Scary.

Is it possible that you're afraid if you tell God you really want to be free He'll bring some girl into your life tomorrow morning and say, "Here she is, son. I've taken you at your word. Marry her"?

The mere idea makes me think of padded cells.

God doesn't operate that way. God knows you far better than you can ever know yourself. Ask Him for *His* view of your limitations. He values His workmanship (you) too much to ever push you beyond safe limits.

The Lord so often spoke of wholeness when He healed. If He "delivers" from doing something He forbids and then does not free us from craving it all the time, we are just not delivered. God expects each of us to commit to Him our subconscious mind, our psychological handcuffs, our uncontrollable desires, and then *He* works. It is the commitment that involves *our* decision.

Are you afraid of losing your identity?

Possibly.

For some of you, in addition to the physical and emotional "benefits" homosexuality brings, there is the comfort that this, at least, makes you outstanding. You feel this is who you are: "I am a homosexual. I'm gay." Are you thinking, "If I release this to God, who will I be?"

Well, who WILL I be?

You are a significant person with certain particular temptations and sins to learn how to overcome, just as I have particular temptations and sins to learn to overcome. Don't confuse your problem of homosexuality with *being*. It's in the realm of doing.

Doing anything can be a danger-fraught path that leads one into the hazy area of lost identity. The compulsive eater *does* something (gorges) until he becomes grossly overweight. His tendency then is not to think, "I am a person of real value and significance who has a weight problem," but, "I *am* unworthy, an unlovable person." His *doing* has led him to confuse who he *is* with his behavior. But doing is *not* being, and while involvement in homosexual acts will certainly cloud a man's concept of himself, I believe that he remains in essence what God made him.

I have a special hope that the Lord will reassure some of you who do not consider yourselves gay but are nagged by doubts about your sexual orientation. You may have succumbed to a seduction scene at one point in your life and you feel branded forever. Many men have had this experience, and it has not affected their basic normal sex orientation. Or you may have no special interest in your own sex, but you're not finding many interesting girls or have gotten the brush-off too many times. Years are slipping by and you are not married and you wonder: "*Am I?* Could I perhaps be. . .?" Remember the differentiation between *doing* and *being* and the element of choice.

At this point someone may say: "It seems to me you are being ridiculously narrow-minded and quite unchristian in the popular understanding of the term. You limit healing to the Christian man? Are you saying Christianity is the only hope? I cannot accept the Christian position."

152

The secular professional outlook for cure seems a bit dim. Dr. Desmond Curran of Great Britain feels that cures in confirmed cases are negligible. Dr. D. Stanley-Jones, also British, thinks it is a moral outrage to attempt to reverse the set patterns and indefensible before the "light of absolute morality." Freud's view was "No cure."

Some therapists are not so gloomy in outlook. Bieber, for example, finds that about 30 percent of those who seek secular counseling find healing.

> Indicative of a favourable prognosis are:
> 1. a wish to change, verbalized at the outset of treatment [notice the element of choice again]
> 2. respect and admiration for one's father
> 3. beginning treatment before the age of 35
> 4. a history of having attempted heterosexual intercourse
> 5. dreams which manifest content depicting heterosexual interest or activity.
>
> Negative prognostic indicators included a history of the mother having openly preferred the patient to her husband and a history of effeminate voice and gestures during childhood.[17]

Some experiments have been made with electroconvulsive therapy, hormones, and hypnosis. These seem to have brought little relief and do nothing at all to alleviate the guilt, which is often the pervading characteristic of the men seeking psychiatric aid for their problem. (Conversely, guilt can be the factor that keeps them from seeking help from anyone.) Even if the guilt is faced, who is to absolve it?

Because I believe Christianity is true, I believe it offers claims worth looking into. Outside the cleansing,

---

[17] Alfred F. Freedman, M.D., Harold I. Kaplan, M.D., Benjamin J. Sadock, M.D., *Modern Synopsis of Comprehensive Textbook of Psychiatry* (Baltimore: Williams and Wilkins Co., 1972), p. 416.

redemptive power of Christ's blood and the great surge of His promised power to change lives, I know of no answer to guilt — not just for homosexuals but for sin and guilt of *any* description.

There *is* such a thing as a fulfilled single life, a life at least relatively free from hunger for the forbidden. Quite a few normal men go through life single, not necessarily wanting to. Their sex drive, too, has to be rechanneled. What was said in chapter 7 about funneling the sex drive into creative effort can apply here. An absorbing interest, a career, a profession, a work God assigns can become a genuine passion.

However, God, well-knowing the power of the drive He has put within His creatures, says, "But if you can't control yourselves, go ahead and marry. It is better to marry than to burn with lust."[18]

Marry!

Two possibilities: abstinence or marriage. To me, this underlines the fact that we may well question the very term "a" homosexual, as if he is constituted a hybrid person, one set apart in *being*. If this were the case, would God be just in giving only two alternatives? Should He not have mentioned a third alternative: homosexual love?

Because you are of such value to Him, He will, *if you allow Him,* deal with one or the other. He can deliver you from uncontrollable, constant hunger or He can bring you to the place of being able to marry. (Don't forget, too, that He can help you understand and deal with all the associated negative influences and fears and empty places that have contributed to your situation today.)

This is deliverance.

---

154   [18] 1 Cor. 7:9.

Have you the courage to ask God to direct you to one woman and think of developing that relationship in *all* its multicolored aspects? If you're willing to risk a relationship with a woman, ask God to help you think of her as a *person*. Trust Him to direct you to someone whom He knows would be empathetic in ways other than the physical: spiritually, culturally, intellectually. Try to discover who she is, while you, the man, take a leadership role in the friendship. Just *because* the friendship is devoid of a strong physical urge, you stand a better chance of getting to know and care about the person. We have distorted the whole concept of the word *love*. Sex is of God, and in His context it's wonderful. But there's an ocean of meaning to love that doesn't involve sex at all. The whole of the Corinthians love chapter has nothing whatever to do with physical love. If you grow to love this one woman you've prayed God to lead you to, you can keep asking God to deal with the physical. God will support your efforts to establish and maintain this relationship beyond your wildest dreams. (And that's almost verbatim from a Christian friend who knows whereof he speaks.)

My teeth are chattering!

Caution: if you are not ready, marriage can be disaster all around. Don't jump into it as a sort of lifeboat or you'll drown and take the lady along. In *any* kind of deeply entrenched, unresolved psychological problem, the love and acceptance of the partner may only add to the guilt.

If you feel you could never stomach marriage and cannot manage sharing a home with another man without strain, what about living alone *but* as part of a loving Christian community? Supportive friendships and activities among people who care about you **155** are important; so is praying with people. Since most gay men are not equally attracted to all men, you should certainly be able to have some godly friendships. *But* — if sex attraction becomes a problem, the friendship had better go, at least until God brings further healing.

Spending much time with the Lord, developing an in-depth relationship with Him, will have much to do with your healing. It should be your top priority. Your life — *yours* — can become one that speaks for God.

The note is *hope!* If homosexuality is sin, it involves *choice* — yours. If there is sin, there is always cleansing and forgiveness.

But I've prayed and felt confident and healed — and then fallen flat. So many times.

Like the rest of us. For every failing Christian there is God's faithfulness, and as we stumble and cry out to Him, again and again He picks us up, dusts us off, and sends us on our way.

I feel so weak.

Good. He has a special message for you: "My power shows up best in weak people."[19]

As I close this long chapter, let me ask you to please believe that I am not saying the solution is *easy*. We have a formidable enemy who knows each of us well and knows just how to make our particular weakness into a tool of destruction. But —

We have a mighty champion, "marching in the greatness of *His* strength," who marches in our defense.

"We are not to look upon ourselves as the . . . sons of slavery under the Law but sons of freedom under

[19] 2 Cor. 12:9.

grace. Plant your feet firmly therefore within the freedom that Christ has won for us, and do not *let yourselves* be caught again in the shackles of slavery."[20]

I pray for each of you that: "The God of hope fill you with all joy and peace in believing, so that by the power of the Holy Spirit you may *abound in hope*."[21]

---

[20] Gal. 4:31; 5:1, Phillips.
[21] Rom. 15:13, RSV.

12

Hardy Perennials: Bachelor's Buttons

Some of you feel you are called to celibacy. Jesus speaks of celibacy as a gift, and any gift of God is valuable. However, it's important for an individual to be sure it *is* God's call and not a cop-out. If it's God's way of life for you, you will be quietly sure and nothing anyone says will make any appreciable difference. But some may be caught in a super-sanctity syndrome. Are you afraid of marriage? Commitment? Sex? Some of you may have so spiritualized the physical that one day you'll find you've corked a teakettle, and teakettles, as James Watt discovered, have explosive potential. Celibacy is not listed under the "gifts of the Spirit" we are told to covet; it seems to be a special gift given to a select few.

I've often wondered how a man knows he is called to be single.

Usually such a man is fully aware of his calling, having chosen it before God with sound reasons for doing so. That type of man needs little help in filling in his time or directing his life. His work is usually consuming, and he sees no room for the obligations of a wife and family. He's learned how to harness his sex drive to produce creativity in other areas; sex, as such, is not a hangup.

However, some of you are single less by conscious choice than by circumstance, procrastination, or fear. You may think wistfully about marriage sometimes, but when confronted with the actual fact (in the shape of a girl who might get serious) you reverse your engines and head for the shore. Is your marriage philosophy summed up in the recent Guinness Ale ad: "I haven't tried it because I don't like it"?

If you have your catch-me-not armor on, if you're off and running (away) when a girl comes along, be careful: You just might run into a solitary-confinement cell. Seems to me much valuable time and energy are spent plotting routes around traps not even set. You may be the stag at bay because of an exaggerated sense of your own value or because of the opposite reason — an exaggerated sense of *lack* of value. Either can be a failure to appropriate *God's* appraisal of your worth.

Some "professional bachelors" may think they're feeding the fires of an old romance when all they're doing is blowing ashes around the room. Others dream of the great girl they're going to find some day. They have clear-cut specifications built on dad's romance with mom, someone else's romance, or a favorite love story. They know just how the girl will look, how old she'll be, her personality, her background. Unreal standards can be another form of cop-out.   159

How so?

If the requirements are made difficult enough, if our man insists he will settle only for *this* particular brand of fair maiden, he is quite safe in his ivory tower. Relying on this secret inner sanctuary, he can ignore reality. Good communication with girls in real situations could be missed completely.

I know a man who spent his life like this. Year after year and girl after girl went by. At seventy-five he was still saying, "Maybe the Lord wants me to get married one of these days." He'd thought about Mary Jane: "Lovely girl but not very neat." Then there was Susan: "Nice but I don't think I could stand her voice." "Martha's too fat — Mabel, too thin. . . ." Usually these women were at least twenty years his junior. The self-delusion is sad. So is the time and energy vaporized in daydreaming instead of becoming a driving force in the man's life.

Of course, one can't marry just "any" girl, but I do see some of you being unrealistic about the girl you imagine right for you. A whole lifetime can slip by! Some of you go off the deep end over girls totally unsuited to the man you are. Some of you are getting older and, over and over, are falling for girls not interested in you at all. Even if you find yourself repeatedly attracted to a certain type, that doesn't mean that's best for you. In fact, some of us have a fatal attraction to just the sort of person most destructive to us. You may be drawn to a clinging vine when what you need is a sturdy sunflower who will be more supportive.

More retiring men are sometimes fascinated by an extroverted speaker-of-the-house type — and end up as a messenger boy. Your heavenly Father knows the girl who can fulfill you and grow *with* you through the years. Ask Him to make you realistic in your views.

Ask Him to show you the girl who will fill needs you may not even realize are there.

Sounds like IBM selection.

Not at all. You can trust God to include the rosy clouds and special sound effects. He's never going to ask you to team up with someone who's just "good for you." He invented love; He's trustworthy. Since He's taken the trouble to number your hairs (diminishing though they may be), He's certainly going to care about something as vital as the right mate.

Do you think prayer always works in the man-woman situation?

Why not?

There have been times when I've really prayed about a girl. In one case I was SURE this was the girl.

And?

She turned me down cold for another Christian guy who had also been praying! So what good did prayer do ME?

Aren't you forgetting *her* right to choose?

But I was so sure it was right.

It may have been. There are these puzzling situations, and it's not evading the issue to say that sometimes there are no clear explanations. One may make a choice that *is* God's will; another person may choose against it. It can hurt.

And even if this has been your experience, God can bring someone else your way. (Surely there's not just one possible mate for each of us. What a frightening thought!) Today you may not feel like considering another girl, but as time goes on and your own development brings growth, you may meet someone quite different who appeals to you and complements the man you have become.

Those of you eyeballing the matrimonial waters but afraid to dive in — are you sure you want to swim? It's no disgrace not to be married. Regrettably, we have romanticized coupleness until it's become a success symbol — the wedding ring replaces the fraternity pin. Some of you bolt at the mere thought of responsibility. Steady on. The single life has some valuable pluses of its own which are relinquished the day you acquire a wife.

Then there's Mr. Popularity. Almost every Christian group seems to have at least one man whose theme song is "Don't Fence Me In." Seasons come and seasons go and he remains a loner, a sort of perpetual male lead in the Bachelor Cotillion. He may be a youth leader, choir director, assistant pastor, general factotum on numerous committees, or just plain Bill Blake. Half the single girls in church flutter their eyelashes at him. To no avail. Meanwhile, our friendly little charm-maker plays "come on" impartially with all of them. He might never think of taking these ladies to bed with him, but unfortunately he never thinks about what's happening to them emotionally, either. He spreads his attentions generously as fancy dictates. The Christian kissing cousin.

To give him his due, he may be partially or even totally unaware of the havoc he creates, but that doesn't lessen his responsibility. Quite apart from the possibility of unfairly raising the hopes or the temperatures of the girls involved, there's a narrow line be-

162

tween this sort of behavior and the two-penny thrill. It's all very subtle, isn't it? The man who is faithful in little things will be faithful in big things.

This type is *not* representative of large numbers of you who are single and who are, like Henry Higgins in *My Fair Lady*, "likely to remain so." Some of you, though, need to come to a clear-cut decision in regard to marriage. Don't seesaw. God can give you real peace about His role for you, but don't overlook the importance of your choice.

If you are interested in marriage, look around you. What are your expectations? Who do you see who fulfills *some* of them? Pray about *that* girl. She may not be God's girl for you, but how will you know unless you talk it over with the Lord? Where the female is concerned, there is no less reliable barometer than your blood pressure. You may be zonked over a girl who'd be so poor a match for you, you'd be aching to trade her in for a new model in a year. But wives aren't sports cars, and the Christian ethic remains "till death do us part."

I have known a couple of men who chose a girl on the basis of her need to be loved. I agree that takes a *big* man, a big faith, and genuine love, but when it happens it's extraordinary.

Some of you are wearing an uneasy singleness but have unresolved problems that need to be worked out. These weeds need clearing off the lot. Have you a mother fixation? Better get it unfixed before you take on a wife. Do you hate your father? No matter how "reasonable" this hate may seem, the fact is that hate is sin. Your part in this duet is to admit it as sin and ask for forgiveness for your own attitude. (God will deal with his.) This is necessary for emotional health, regardless of marital status.

This is not hard; it's impossible unless you include God. He says, "*I will give you a new heart. . . .*" Only 163

God can do a guaranteed heart transplant. The point is, are you willing to let Him?

Forgiveness has been called "remembrance without ill feeling." To forgive others, even to accept their forgiveness, we have to accept God's forgiveness. If we remain unhealed before God, forgiveness from others will only push us to deeper despair. In a marriage, this becomes a powder keg that can ignite and blast a marriage to Reno.

Do you think a single person can live a really fulfilled life?

Life being the imperfect thing it is, there is no such thing as perfect fulfillment. The unmarried man may be lonely and wish he had a family; the married man may envy the bachelor's freedom to paint pictures all day and half the night.

Christ spoke of men who choose singleness for the Kingdom's sake. We all know gifted, attractive men who have had many opportunities for marriage but who feel God wants them single. They're busy, fulfilled men. Lonely moments? Of course. But fulfillment? Certainly. A single man has greater freedom than the family man. He's often mobile. He can become more involved with others. He may have more time for study, prayer, for spreading himself over a wider area. All those things contribute to fulfillment.

There are plenty of activities waiting for a single man to get involved in. Working with boys is rewarding, and today's kids often need a father or brother image. Sports are a great social outlet. Some of you are musical. Play your guitar. Or what about that voice you've been bouncing against the bathroom tiles? Maybe God has a use for it. Some are interested in other arts.

164 Hobbies can develop into a number of things: social

door-openers, antidotes for loneliness, or — who knows — maybe a living?

Are you doing things for other people? Have you shared what you now have: car, apartment, gifts, your free time? Sharing is a learned process for most of us. Opening the home you have now is a rewarding experience. You don't need a wife to entertain well. Men make fabulous cooks. Don't like to cook? Find a friend who enjoys helping out in the culinary department. Or get hot pastrami on rye from the corner delicatessen.

Some of you may be older and find that flexibility comes harder. Whether you marry or not, those ingrained habit patterns can block your creativity in living. Do you always have dinner at 7:00? Can't think of missing certain TV shows? Hate interruptions in your tidy schedule? The walls may close in one day, and you'll be dead for lack of air. An open, two-way communication with the Lord which leads to openness with people and life is the best way for us to avoid spinal rigidity and atrophy of the imagination.

Enjoy friendships on an easy level without demands, possessiveness, or exaggerated fears. Don't be afraid that helping a girl move from one apartment to another or taking her to a concert is a declaration of intent.

At any age, you may not feel your talent is conversation. Good listeners are always in demand. Rarer than rubies they are, and people need someone who will really *hear* what they're saying.

Many of you are already into the listening bit, counseling young people. In spiritual counseling, you are dealing on the deepest level of human personality. You quickly cut through externals and a close bond can grow between the two involved. In the case of a man-woman confrontation, the person being counseled may become attached to the counselor. Whether it's an attempt to introduce the girl to Christianity, help a **165**

Christian with her problems, or give individual studies, the line between the counsel offered and the counselor himself becomes blurry. A dependency relationship begins to grow and real emotional damage can result.

Put it like this: A man starts helping a girl to understand Christianity. What could be better? They have talks, Bible studies, and pray together. Both are as sincere as they know how to be. Meanwhile, the girl's admiration for the man grows. (This is tricky because it's such a genuinely innocent activity. Nobody expects a booby trap at a Bible study.) Perhaps the girl even becomes a Christian under his guidance. One fine day our girl says, "This is it! Since God has used this man to help me so much, he must be my dream man." Trouble at the crossroads — because *he* has no such ideas. Now what? He'll be a fortunate man if *all* that happens is that the girl is emotionally hurt. That's far from negligible, but a more serious result can be that her pain and confusion will cause her to dump the whole idea, the truth along with the friendship that "betrayed" her.

But if she really became a Christian?

Because of the intricacy of emotions the two things still can become inextricably mixed. There may come a day of doubt even later, and she may begin to wonder how much was God and how much was the man.

Well now, look here. A girl comes to me with questions. Say a girl interested in becoming a Christian. What do I say: "Go away, little girl. I'm a man and you're a girl and we can't talk"?

Hardly that. But if you feel she is genuinely interested after a talk or two, send her to someone older or to a woman or girl you know. Incidentally, this is a sure way to find what she's really interested in: the truth or you.

Of course, *you* can be the one who gets caught, and then your usefulness to her on a spiritual plane is just about over. Please consider this carefully, won't you? I've seen so much misunderstanding and hurt come out of this kind of "good" situation that I have come to regard it as one of the enemy's subtlest tools.

Do you think the same thing applies for married women?

Married women aren't invulnerable nor are you. People are people, and temptation doesn't depart at the altar. There's no armor that keeps you and the married woman from being attracted. It could, in fact, develop into a worse situation since, potentially, more people are involved. I think the same reasoning applies here as with a single girl.

In the long run, the amount of fulfillment experienced in any life is due to a great degree to the individual himself. I do not believe God wants even one of His children to lead a sterile, uninteresting life. How could He, when He Himself said, "I came to bring them life, and far more life than before."[1]

So, if you're a bachelor today and think it's your calling, be happy in it. But don't just develop bachelor syndrome from fear or indecision. If you do want to marry, be realistic in your expectations.

And let God heal the past.

Whether you are committed to bachelorhood or hoping for marriage, accept each day as a challenge in creative living. Today is a link being forged in the chain of eternity. It counts.

---

[1] John 10:10, Phillips.

13

Men Who Stand Tall

In today's kaleidoscopic world there is a recognized need for leaders. This need was articulated in a *Time* article which decried the mediocrity in national and international leadership in all countries. The article saw little hope for much change unless "history" delivers us some unknowns on white chargers.[1]

What *Time* has to say about lack of leadership in the contemporary political field is reflected in other areas. What constitutes leadership? Alexander the Great, Caesar, Paul, Napoleon, Luther, Lincoln, Churchill, de Gaulle — each left a notable imprint on history because he passionately *believed* in something. He stood firmly on that belief, right or wrong, and was able to influence thousands — in some cases, millions.

There have always been leaders. The idea of hierarchy has a divine origin. Even before the creation of our universe and man, there was Satan, the anointed cherub, beautiful and powerful. When he fell, he drew

---

[1] *Time*, 21 January 1974.

many with him, the "evil rulers of the unseen world, those mighty satanic beings and great evil princes of darkness who rule this world; and . . . huge numbers of wicked spirits in the spirit world."[2] Michael and Gabriel, the archangels, possess immense power, and Scripture speaks of a great host of heavenly beings.

Back of these is God.

After the Fall, when man declared his rebellious independence of God, he began setting up his own leaders. The power struggle began with Cain, and from then on leaders — good, bad, and indifferent — have come and gone. Without God, the human being has trouble with power. That "power corrupts and total power corrupts totally" is the bitter lesson history tries to teach us.

Not realizing that the cavity inside is God-shaped, people often run panting after the man or woman who comes as purveyor of answers to the big questions of life. When a new voice promises something better, they swing in that direction.

In my childhood Dr. Emmett Holt Sr. had held the field for years as the leading child specialist. Children were to be treated firmly, not fondled or indulged. Many of your generation are Spock products, whose mothers followed Dr. Spock as if he'd invented babies. Today Spock himself is retracting his teachings. Whether or not the Skinner box will ever become really popular remains to be seen.

In the contemporary art field no one person had as great an impact as the late Pablo Picasso. The stormy Spaniard who progressed from the realism shown in Barcelona's Picasso museum to the grotesque images of his ninth decade had more influence on art than anyone else who lived in this century. But he is gone, and someone else will bring new theories, draw new fol-

---

[2] Eph. 6:12.

lowers, though it may well be a long time before anyone of his luminosity arrives.

In a short space of time your generation has seen the impact of the Beatles and the Rolling Stones give way before the Jefferson Airplane and the Grateful Dead. And already, *these* groups are remembered more for their past than their present contributions to the rock scene.

In religion, young people, repelled by the sterility of organized churchianity, have followed the Pied Pipers of Hinduism and other Eastern thought. First, the Maharishi, profiting greatly by his association with the Beatles, drew thousands to his expensive Shangri-la in the Himalayas. Others followed. Now it is the young Guru Maharajji whose Cadillac is kissed and who brings the promise of peace in our time.

Always man seeks answers to his questions of *Who am I? Why am I here? Where am I going?* Always he follows someone who promises to have the ability to assuage his fears and meet his deep needs: financial security, emotional security, self-fulfillment, inner peace. And an answer to death.

There is in all of us a deep need for purpose in life, a goal worth dying for. Part of communism's success is that it gives people a chance to wholly commit themselves. In an era where such opportunities are rare, it offers people a cause for which to risk their lives.

Admitting the failures of the church and our dismal non-involvement where the action really is, what has Christianity to offer? What do we have to say to confused modern man who sees little meaning in life in general and his own in particular?

For those of us who believe that there is Truth and that God lives, this is certainly not the time to sit down and join in the Greek chorus of despair. Neither can we join in the bacchanal of "eat, drink, and be merry for tomorrow we die." Direct descendants in the royal line of believers, we are involved in the greatest of all causes. History *is* going somewhere, and the Christian has answers. This makes our responsibility overwhelming.

To non-believing man such claims sound not only preposterous but revoltingly conceited, which they are if there is no truth. However, since we are convinced of God's existence, of His self-revelation in the incarnation of Jesus Christ, and in His Word, let's stop being insular, stop being defensive. Let's proclaim that God *is* by living out our faith in such a joyous way people will be drawn to Him. A small band of men were called those "who have turned the world upside down."[3] Are we doing any globe-turning? Is our living making any impact on our world, our nation, even on our urban, suburban, or scholastic neighborhood?

Those of you reading this book: bank clerk, student, craftsman, philosopher, disillusioned divorcé, dissatisfied drop-out, or successful professional man — whoever you are, you have a calling to be committed to a great cause which is going somewhere. Many of you are potential leaders. *All* of you can choose to make some impact on your environment. For some of you the field is broad. On the other hand, some of you are quiet men with no talent for speaking in public or writing or creating masterpieces. No matter. If you allow God to ignite your mind, to show you why He chose *you, He will use you.* Since He has chosen to entrust His message to men, not angels, He needs each of us. He calls some to go a long way from home, but He uses all kinds of men to do things in all sorts of places. The spread of Christianity began with a small group of average men. Whatever assignment He gives you, it will be custom-made to the person you are.

In our era was have made a god of public opinion,

---

[3] Acts 17:6, RSV.

and we sacrifice our convictions on its altar. What the majority does or believes *is*. The seeping poison of the "God-is-dead" school, or the even deadlier "so-what" school, has come into the living rooms of the world, into tiny villages in Switzerland, into skyscraper hotels in Tokyo, into remote farm houses, hospital wards, and prisons. Evolution and determinism are presented with no margin given to the thousands of well-educated dissidents to these theories. Never before have so many been so manipulated by so few. A Christian may feel squashed or he may begin to doubt his own conclusions. We need to remember something the brilliant, non-Christian scientist Jacob Bronowski has said: "Every judgement in science stands upon the edge of error and is personal."[4] Think that through before you accept the latest scientific pronouncement as if it were a divine fiat.

In order to make any dent in the monolith of anti-God thinking, we must be well-rooted in Truth. Our personal faith may be comforting, but if we think subconsciously of God as a White, Anglo-Saxon Protestant, if we forget His magnificence and His control over the complexity of His universe, we will be dazzled by the theories that confront us. We need His perspective, and in His statements in Scripture we *have* that perspective as a straight edge. Daring? It's a revolutionary claim. Do we believe it or not?

The splintering power within the atom, the well-ordered activity within cells, the numbing vastness of space should all add to our adoration of their designer. The Old Testament men who addressed God as "maker of heaven and earth and all that is in them" did not understand that "all" as well as we do, but they knew God.

---

[4] Jacob Bronowski, *The Ascent of Man* (Boston: Little Brown and Co., 1974).

As men look into the "peepholes of eternity," they can marvel that God has created them with minds that can crack open cosmic secrets and that tiny man is of such significance to Him. Instead of curling up in an apologetic ball, we Christians should be living lives that are shouts of praise.

Today's battle is being fought in the thought world. How much does your life influence the thought life of others? Some Christians don't seem aware that there's a war on. We are actively engaged or passively indifferent. None of us is a cipher. The scary reality is that if we are not positively engaged for God, we are by default contributing to the other side, the side against God.

In the battle for men's minds, God looks for leaders. Many of you are young men. The leaders from whom you have learned are growing older. Every day life becomes more like a super highway with all markers removed. Your challenge is to set up some well-lighted directional signals. Are you ready for all this involves? It means being willing to equip your mind to deal with today's thinking, to learn how to communicate God's ageless, changeless truth in language your contemporaries will understand.

Many of you, well-fortified with Scripture, wonder why you cannot "get through" to modern man in his despair and confusion. How can you if you don't know what he's thinking? You do not go to a foreign country to teach math or history without learning the language of that country. No matter how well-equipped you are technically, you won't get off square one till you can communicate. We are slow to admit that our familiar evangelical terminology is often so much technical jargon that conveys nothing to the twentieth century mind. We say, "God loves you" to someone; his mind may stumble over the word *love,* let alone the word *God.* We know who we mean when we say God, but for 173 him the word may conjure up a dozen different possibilities: a nebulous power, the first cause, an experience, a philosophic other, the God-behind-God, a zero. And if he has no idea who God is, how can we talk to him about God's Son?

We tell him Christ died for his sins. His whole psychological orientation may deny the fact that such a thing as moral guilt exists. Insisting he must say "God be merciful to me, a sinner" at this point is a bit like beating a blind man over the head because he won't swear a cat is black.

These are only two examples of the mentality around you. As God's man, learn to define your terms and to know the possible definitions the other person may have for those same terms.

Know where the war is going on. The battlefronts today are bewilderingly complex. There's immorality, the amused tolerance of "ordinary" promiscuity, and almost any kind of deviant sexual behavior. Involved with this is the dissolution of the home.

Another front is the drug culture, possibly receding but definitely still there. The demonic and occult permeate more deeply into a wider segment of society than many realize or perhaps want to realize. Deterministic psychology and relativistic thinking influences the lives of many who never heard the terms. (A man need not be a deep thinker to absorb these things if he watches TV, reads his paper, looks at ads on buses or underground, or listens to his car radio.) Finally, esoteric religions of many stripes are reaching middle-class suburbanites as well as trendy intellectuals.

We need to be able to analyze, sift, clarify today's destructive philosophies. As they infiltrate our thinking in their more insidious forms — comedy shows, brilliant films, best sellers, scientific journals, and slanted news reports — we need to be aware of what's happening inside our own heads.

174

Within the whole spectrum of Christian thinking (genuine and counterfeit) there are the fronts of liberal theology which undermine the validity of the Scriptures, of emotional religious experiences without content, and of a strange militant kind of authoritarianism.

While we deplore fanaticism, let's be prayerfully aware of how far we dare yield before we must say, "Thus far and no farther." Tolerance is good until it becomes lack of conviction.

With so many battles proliferating, the need for dedicated leadership is painfully obvious.

What characterizes a Christian leader?

Christ Himself said: "Whoever wants to be great among you must be your servant."[5] A Christian leader places himself under Christ's leadership, subservient to the authority of Scripture and the guidance of the Holy Spirit. How many individuals or organizations wait before God for their direction? How many take on leadership in a humanistic way so that they, not the Holy Spirit, are the directors of their lives and work?

When people vacillate and lack conviction, a man of strong convictions may easily assume leadership. When there *are* many such people, Satan is only too happy to supply leaders from his roster.

While the need for courageous leaders is great, it is dangerous to *seek* leadership. Not only is there the risk of not being qualified, but leaders will be judged by a stiffer standard.[6] Let God do the choosing, but be *willing* to be chosen.

There is always the question of ability. Since He designed you and gave you your abilities, He will put you

---

[5] Mark 10:43.
[6] James 3:1, Phillips.

in the right place — in fact, the *best* place. Once you assess what your abilities are, there is a responsibility to develop and improve them.

Two poles are dangerous here: Some of you have so little belief in yourself (and perhaps in God?) that you are closed to possibilities — perhaps blind to the gifts He has given. Others of you are trying to succeed in an area for which you have little gift. If you want to be shown, God will let you know if you've gotten off the track.

There are other dangers besides lack of ability — lack of calling, pride, extremism, and the frightening human ability of attracting people to ourselves rather than to the Lord. A Christian leader has deeper need than most men for a whole battalion of people who will pray for him consistently and seriously.

God's leaders need conviction as to the inspiration of the whole Bible. Today there is a chipping away at the foundations. If we are *not* backed by the verbal revelation of God, we have no final authority for anything and soon must move into the camp of the agnostics.

A leader needs a life that fits his talk and a willingness to break with sin. (*Willingness* is the operative word.) A dichotomy between personal life and public role won't go. A man who is strong and loving to the world in general and a tyrant at home is unstable, and one day the laminated surface will crack and the sad hypocrisy show through.

Will you be men of vision, of sanctified imagination — men willing to attempt new things? You young men have the challenge of establishing new traditions (not new theology, but new ways of doing things: new ways of communication, new approaches, new music, new art). It takes courage to break with established
176 ways and a willingness to prayerfully separate the

biblical concepts which we must not change from the "Shallow answers built on men's thoughts and ideas."

Above everything else, God's leaders need love. Not just in outward demonstration but inside. The corrosive hate, personal bitterness, envy, and resentment must go.

Love. For God first, then for people. Love from the heart, the core of things. Preaching, teaching, sharing, counseling — all need the climate of genuine concern.

Godly leadership includes availability and flexibility. Have you areas of yes-butness (I'll do this, go there *but* — not *that* place, not *this* person, not *that* assignment)?

Time is involved. Lots of it. And work — that not-always-popular ethic. And enthusiasm. You can't get people away from the starting gate if you yourself are not sparked.

"God's people must not be quarrelsome; they must be gentle, patient teachers of those who are wrong. Be humble when you are trying to teach those who are mixed up concerning the truth. For if you talk meekly and courteously to them they are more likely, with God's help, to turn away from their wrong ideas and believe what is true."[7] Are these our attitudes at home, on campus, in the office, in the shop, in Fleet Street, or on Capitol Hill? Or are we militant, argumentative, or dogmatic in a "good cause"?

If God offers you a position of leading others, you have a price to pay if you accept it. Your home life will suffer. You will have less time for your family and friends. Your "own" time will dwindle and sometimes be nonexistent. Your strength may be used up until you are ready to throw in the towel. Your career may change; some personal dreams may go. It may mean a break with materialism. Since that is the integration

---

[7] 2 Tim. 2:24, 25.

point for many, you may need willingness to demonstrate it isn't yours. Loss of status, job, income, rejec-
tions that hurt — all these things are potentially on the
price tag.

It is vital that leaders be men of prayer. Not just men
who pray, but men whose lives and outlooks are permeated with prayer. There should be a persistent thirst
in us that is only slaked by communication with our
Father.

Do we really believe prayer has an effect on history,
that something will happen when we pray or will fail
to happen if we do not pray? We need to so value
prayer as a weapon against the powers of darkness
that we are willing to give much time to "just praying." This is an instrument for the coming of God's
kingdom. (How many of us believe that kingdom will
come? Do we want it to come?) We are surrounded
by strikes, corruption, diplomatic mumbo-jumbo, violence. God says we are to pray for governments. Are
we obedient?

Genuine moral and intellectual courage is needed
to stand against the rising wall of antagonism to biblical Christianity. There may well come a time for
physical courage. It is true today in such countries as
China, Rumania, Russia. Why should we think we
will be exempt? We applaud the blazing courage of
Solzhenitsyn, but have we asked ourselves, "If it came
to that, how would *I* stand as a lone Christian?"

"The value of a thing to you is determined by how
much you are willing to pay for it."

14

A Sound of Trumpets

"The individual in today's society might as well be in a pinball machine. Virtually everything in society effects his life, yet for the most part, he is almost powerless to cope with it. The future shock phenomenon just accelerates the changes."[1]

Whether you are going to be a leader in a big way, a small way, or not at all, the fact remains that each Christian has his own special place, one no one else is qualified to fill as well. He is God's light. Shining doesn't take talent, just a willingness to be consumed.

You may have few talents, but whoever you are, wherever you live, you have a life style. Consciously chosen or drifted into, your way of life says much about who you are and about the reality of things you believe. Will it recommend itself as an alternative to today's materialism or will people see only a "Christianized" version of the Establishment? Is your mode

---

[1] *Saturday Review,* May 1973.

of living visibly creative, a negation of media pressures, a refusal to be manipulated? Are you living out your own personal revolution against commercialism, or can people say, "So what's different about *your* life style? Talk is cheap"?

In one sense, there is no such thing as a *Christian* life style. The kind of home you have, how many cars, your wardrobe, whether you have a job or are in "Christian service" — all these things depend on God's leading of the individual. However, with the consensus stressing the acquisition of things, we Christians need to consider ways and means of living so our lives will challenge the status quo. Can we set an alternative life style for people who are either sick of society's values or anesthetized into a numbness in which they are only vaguely aware of "something wrong"?

The hippie culture which brought such animosity from parents had the advantage of reacting against standards it saw as going nowhere. If, the kids reasoned, a college education was only going to qualify them for a job to make more money to buy a grander house and drive a bigger car, why bother? In many cases their parents were alcoholics, swingers, or simply querulously dissatisfied with life, sans direction or achievement. Then, why college? "Success"? Who needed it? They had an abundance of things at home, but too often they also had a dearth of communication and love. Their difficulty lay in having no strong alternatives. They knew what to revolt against but not what to rally to.

We must not be guilty of the same thing. In England and in the U.S. many Christians seem caught in a life style that exhibits little that is different from the norms of the affluent, society. A small minority think one way of being heard is dissent from this way of living. Fair enough, but what's the alternative? If we do deplore

180 conformity, what have we to offer?

It's easy to become polarized in an attempt to answer these questions. To lay down rules — "How One Must Live in the New Christian Society" — is to inhibit individual freedom before God. But an every-man-for-himself philosophy is the antithesis of Christ's teaching.

What are the alternatives? This is a subject that should be taking up much more of our time and thinking than it is. Groups of you men might discuss ways to beat a technological take-over of home life, ways to avoid a sterile conformity, ways of living that would reflect the kind of freedom we believe God gives a man who has been brought into the right relationship with Him.

Two words are important: *simplicity* and *beauty*. In the past some Christians have tried to live "differently." They did this by excising anything not absolutely essential to life. What emerged was something harsh and unlovely which, more than *self*-denial, was denial of the God who filled His universe with so much beauty: stars, snowflakes, flowers, grasses — above all — people. To search *only* for beauty, conversely, has led to an insulated, hedonistic existence.

For the Christian, then, the quest is one for equilibrium — a life of simplicity that is also beautiful. Easy? The search for the simple life has become a complicated problem.

Experts trained in fostering the gospel of discontent bombard us with more complex ways to "simplify our living." Even many "labor-saving" devices, intended to eliminate drudgery, require large initial monetary outlay, expensive repairs, and speedy replacement. What is worse, they often rob us of the joy of creativity.

For example: You may be driving a big new car these days, but has anything ever given you the satisfaction you got from that first car you all but glued together? Or take sophisticated power tools. Granting their value for heavy cutting or for repetitive tasks, **181** are they a satisfying substitute for the tactile enjoyment of hand-rubbing wood, the creative pleasure of putting something of yourself into the object you're making? Some machinery has a place in everyone's life, but we need to be careful we're not regressing from being creative dreamers to gadgeteers.

Where is our creative bankruptcy more apparent than in our inability to have meaningful, interesting conversation? Much of our entertainment is manufactured. We live vicariously. Watching flowers grow or animals develop on film is educational, but it cannot take the place of touching, smelling, owning.

Personal interchange has become mechanized. The simple act of grocery shopping used to involve an exchange between people who knew one another. In England one still can shop at the local butcher's, the small vegetable shop, the bakery, the fish market, but in the U.S. it's become a racing foray into vast food arsenals and on to the drive-in bank. I sometimes wonder about the solitary people, especially the old. Buying their food used to bring social contact. Now they must roam confusing Babbitt-warrens to buy their pint of milk and some cheese.

Back to the eighteenth century, Gini?

No. I am not unaware of the beneficial advances in many fields: the mitigation of suffering through modern medicine; sheer drudgery exchanged for more free time or creative work; the marvel of fast travel. (It's an exercise in creative thinking just to know how to *use* the bonus of more free time.)

What is your top priority? Is it the job? That's usually first consideration, isn't it? A man is trained as a teacher, a philosopher, an artist, a mechanic, a bank 182 clerk. Single or married, his first consideration is,

"Where can I get the best financial return for this skill or profession I have?" It's so universally accepted as the logical approach that one does not even consider another way.

But the Christian is here on earth for something more than being a mechanic, a bank clerk, a businessman, or whatever.

Even for something more than being the best mechanic, bank clerk, or businessman?

That's certainly important. However, within whatever category our work brings us, we are here for communication and fellowship with our Creator. We are also here to exhibit the truth and beauty we believe to be an integral part of God's world. We are here to share what we have with others (not *only* the Gospel, but ourselves, our talents, our homes). If these things are top priority, our jobs, our families, and our friendships will be in right perspective. We will look for God's direction how and where our lives can demonstrate our conviction that God *is*.

Conviction can be costly. It could mean a job with less pay if the higher salaried slot involved business practices morally wrong or destructive to what man really is. It could mean living in a city when a man prefers a farm. It could mean moving to an uncongenial climate to be near a Christian community.

Increasingly, Christian community is becoming more than an experiment for the imaginative few; it is becoming a necessity. The spiritual and ideological warfare around us is too strong for an individual or family to cope with alone. A Sunday service and weekly Bible study are not enough. We need the community for warmth and support; we may soon need it for survival. 183

What kind of community?

It would vary according to location, types of people, interests. I am not thinking primarily of a commune: that is, people working and living under one roof. This kind of community has a definite place, but there is a need for something more permanent with wider appeal.

Such as?

A group of Christians, covering the whole generation spectrum, committed to one another, living near each other.

A church?

A church would probably be the nerve-center of such a community. It's hard to visualize a Christian community without a core of worship and fellowship centered in Bible-based teaching and much prayer. One could imagine more than one church, if the size of the community warranted it. Each could have a slightly different emphasis. As you start thinking along these lines, you're going to come up with some novel and challenging ideas (which I hope you'll write me about).

Herewith some possibilities for you to consider: Think of such a community as a wheel with many spokes radiating from the church as its center — the spokes being clusters of people with some common interests. One U.S. community has gradually placed its people in old apartment houses in a relatively inexpensive section of the city. As one apartment is vacated, word gets around and soon another family or single from the community moves in. The non-184 Christians in the building may be attracted by the corporate demonstration of practical Christianity. The model is freer than a church structure, allowing for more individuality and a wide variety of leadership. The style of community, the kinds of activities would emanate from the needs and types of individuals involved.

Imagine a group of people interested in the graphic arts rapping one night a week, discussing trends, sorting out problems. Or writers in different fields bouncing ideas around. Crafts people, cabinet makers, or weavers could meet.

Sounds folksy.

I'm not talking about busywork. I see the community in terms of eventual survival. Making one's own cloth or bread or furniture may one day be a necessity. The community's aim could be to be self-sustaining. Not everyone likes to dig in vegetable gardens, not everyone is good at it, but there could be communal garden plots such as one sees in England or outside European cities. Those of you who like to garden might agree to plant and share and the whole community would profit.

Musicians might meet regularly and perform for the fun of it: folk, pop, or Beethoven quartets. We've nearly lost the art of informal music making. A group of amateurs won't sound like professionals, but you'll never get the same creative thrill out of listening to music that you get from making your own. Music making may not be a survival technique, but it's a healing thing for those making it as well as for those who listen.

Do you have time to do all the reading you want to? It could be interesting to pool your reading on current events or any particular subject and discuss it. Sessions where interesting tapes were heard, discussions per se 185 or after lectures can be stimulating. (If the community had a space expert, a professional man, a sculptor, each could talk on his speciality.)

Film forums make a good focal point. A few people see an important film, then gather afterwards to discuss it and pray about its effect.

An attractive room where lonely people would feel free to drop in could be planned. One or two people could be there for them to talk to. (Not, in the first instance, to talk to *them* — a big difference. Who this man is, why he came, what he is actually saying — these must take precedence over zealous anxiety to *tell* him something.) Availability is important. "By appointment only" is a heart-stopper to someone whose need is *now*. Many of you single men know too well what loneliness is. You can ease your own pain as you reach out a hand to others. For example, you could help staff a phone service for distress calls. (This would also be a fine way to utilize the wisdom of older people, even those not very mobile.)

The needs of the larger community should concern Christians. Is it enough to thank God for our well-cooked meals and then just ask Him to "bless the hungry"? Dare we stop there? What about setting apart a percentage of what we spend on food each shopping trip for those who are in short supply? It wouldn't hurt us to go without a meal now and then and put the cost in the kitty. Another way to tackle the problem might be to assess the value of that second helping or the dessert you don't need and forego it, putting the value aside. This might strike you as ridiculously little, but the box will fill up quickly, and you will have improved your waistline in the bargain. You can depend on God's showing you *where* to use such money if you just have some for Him to use.

You single men would make a special contribution
186 to the kind of community we're discussing. You're

often in the middle of creative activity and are asking challenging questions. An urban situation might well have more singles than couples.

Too often, as you know, a single feels out of the center of things in church setups. If the church sometimes fails them, the business world is wide-awake to the needs of unrooted people. The sharp-eyed entrepreneurs of mammon are capitalizing on the singles market to the tune of jingling cash registers. What happens to the personhood of those involved is no concern of theirs.

Are you advocating Christian singles' complexes?

Quite the contrary! Even in an urban community the mixture of single and married, of differing age groups is good; each group learns from and enriches the other. But if we don't take the social and emotional needs of single people more seriously, we leave many of them hungry for the promotional lures that come attractively baited. We need to think through the problem and come up with good alternatives to answer the real needs of the large numbers of Christian singles. And who is better equipped than you are to produce some innovations?

Individuals dedicated to helping new Christians grow are an important part of a Christian community. Personally, I prefer the one-to-one ratio if possible — or at least very small groups. But you may like large classes.

Bible study and prayer groups are familiar but sometimes static. One idea: a group dedicated to pray for Christians all over the world who are in prison, or who have no Bibles and live in fear of punishment just for being Christians. (In Russia, groups of believers have been tracked down even to forest retreats where they have been beaten. If I were in such circumstances, I'd **187** surely hope someone was praying for me!) In the beginning you might feel odd, praying for people you know nothing about. Experiment. You'll find it advancing in scope. You'll hear news about imprisoned or threatened Christians and soon you'll find yourself wishing you had more time to pray. "Don't forget about those in jail. Suffer with them as though you were there yourself."[2]

Your Bible study could be aimed at the need of a particular group or, again, at survival.

Survival Bible study?

Do we English and American Christians seriously consider that one day we ourselves may face the situation that confronts believers in iron and bamboo curtain countries — no Bibles? Somewhere in the back of our minds we agree that — maybe — sometime — but we don't really believe it. If we did, we'd be doing something about it.

Like?

Memorizing. Oh, we all have dandy excuses at hand for not memorizing: "I'm content to get the meaning. . . . I can't memorize. . . . I thought that was for kids. . . . I'm too busy. . . . I'm too tired. . . . I'm too lazy." (*That* one's honest at least.) Spend ten minutes thinking what your own life would be like if you had *no* Bible, not one page, not a printed verse anywhere.

The sort of memory work I'm talking about is a long-term project. A memorizing session could be incorporated into Bible studies. You could check each other out and encourage each other. It's hard work. In a

[2] Heb. 13:3.

more or less permanent community, people could memorize different sections. One takes a psalm, another part of Colossians, another chooses separate verses he likes. One thing I'm sure of: You will find this a genuine enrichment of your life right *now*. One day it might be not only your solace but your sanity. (During the imprisonments in Korea it was found that the men who knew God's Word came off surprisingly well; they had a positive weapon against brainwashing.)

Another vital part of living together would be extended periods of prayer with or without fasting. This can be a corporate or an individual effort. If a general gathering were impractical, people might just set aside a special day or half-day and pray where they chose.

The time factor's tough.

I don't deny it, but most of us manage to find time for the things we really want to do. A day or even a half-day a month set aside for prayer pays bigger dividends than we know.

Creative Christian living often includes an open home. We are not permitted airtight compartments. What often cracks the veneer of a non-believer is not "testimonies" or "witnessing" but love expressed in welcoming hospitality. Not just a hospitality of comfortable "equals." Is your door open to barefoot, blue-jeaned long-hairs? To the man or girl whose skin is a different shade than yours? Are you thinking: "But after *all* — my apartment house, the people at the desk — what would the neighbors think? I might lose my lease." You might, at that. Are you prepared to be *that* loving, *that* hospitable? Are you ready for the great adventure of showing the love and warmth of the Lord Jesus Christ in practical ways, in ways even the most frightened rebel can understand? These are the implications of "given to hospitality." *You* may be the 189 long-haired one who wouldn't consider asking the upper-middle-class man with his suit and tie to come to your home. A risk? Yes, there's a risk. All creative adventure involves risk. (Again the word of caution: Not every temperament can handle this phase of sharing. The girl you marry — or you yourself — *may* be without this gift. We do not all fit one mold.)

Let your "sanctified imaginations" go and ask God for ideas. There are communities of various kinds already in existence whose ideas you can benefit from without becoming carbon copies.

Technology is a Colossus that straddles the world, and the individual is only making a Lilliputian noise. Bible-believing Christians are a small minority. As people become reduced to numbers controlled by levers and push buttons, you who believe your first allegiance is to the personal God are going to be increasingly unpopular. Many of you may be asked to stand up and be counted when the standing up will be costly.

I do not think I exaggerate. The overture for the Brave New World is already playing; the lights are dimmed. The actors waiting in the wings are not going to be any more in sympathy with Christ's followers than was the power bloc in the first century.

The danger could be the KGB knocking at the door at midnight; but even greater is the danger of the subliminal infiltration going on, with the termites of an overfed indifference already hollowing out the foundation of our faith. Dry rot comes unnoticed. If you are faced with the need for defending your beliefs, will your spiritual muscles have atrophied from disuse? Sometimes it takes a grittier brand of courage to stand against the consensus, to live for your beliefs, than to face a gas chamber or a firing squad. Most of us are not nearly as much in danger of being thrown to the lions as of keeping the lions for house pets.

190

It is important to assess the dangers, but that is the dark side of the stage. If we see only that, we can be overwhelmed. On the opposite side, the light is very bright. When Christ left this earth, He told the weak little group He left behind that He had all authority and that "those who believe shall use my authority."[3] He challenged these men to spread the news. Quite aware of what He was asking, He threw down the gauntlet without qualification. Two thousand years later He remains the Unconquered, the Unconquerable, and He has promised to come back.

The prophesied return of Christ is going to be historically fulfilled as surely as the prophecies of His first coming. One night in a Jewish town the thousands of years of prophecy had an end and — He was there: a real baby in a real cattle stall on real straw. The sounds and smells in that shed were no different than those in any other cattle shed that night — except that a baby cried. There's going to come a day that can be marked on the calendar, when life will be going along as usual: newscasts, programs on TV, commuters going to work, housewives sending the kids off to school, cars jamming the road, people getting married, others being buried, and — He will be here.

> The Lord himself will come down from heaven with a mighty shout and with the soul-stirring cry of the archangel and the great trumpet-call of God. And the believers who are dead will be the first to rise to meet the Lord. Then we who are still alive and remain on the earth will be caught up with them in the clouds to meet the Lord in the air and remain with him forever.[4]

Under the banner of this coming King, go forward. Go with singing and shouting and a sound of trumpets. Sons of freedom!

---

[3] Mark 16:17.
[4] 1 Thess. 4:16, 17.